basketry & weaving
with natural materials

basketry & weaving
with natural materials

PAT DALE

Kangaroo Press

DEDICATION

I would like to acknowledge

- Douglas Fuchs, a visiting New York basket maker, for sowing the seed;
- Country Women of Australia for my introduction to natural basketry;
- Basket makers, crafts colleagues and students for encouragement and support;
- My husband and family for putting up with the fire hazard at the back door; and
- Mary Ellis who typed and checked my manuscript material and nourished the seed until it blossomed. My special thanks.

BASKETRY & WEAVING WITH NATURAL MATERIALS

First published in Australia and New Zealand in 1998 by Kangaroo Press
An imprint of Simon & Schuster Australia
20 Barcoo Street, East Roseville NSW 2069

Reprinted in 2002

A Viacom Company
Sydney New York London Toronto Tokyo Singapore

© Pat Dale 1998

National Library of Australia
Cataloguing-in-Publication data

Dale, Pat, 1938-.
 Basketry & weaving with natural materials.

 Includes index.
 ISBN 0 86417 914 6.

 1. Basket making. 2. Weaving. 3. Textile crafts. 4. Textile fibres - Identification. 5. Nature craft. 6. Handicraft. I. Title.

746.41

COVER: Basket by Pat Dale made from wisteria vine and Dianella (native flax)
PHOTOGRAPHERS: Pat Dale, David Starkey, Mary Ellis and Trevor Foon

Set in 10/12pt Sabon
Printed in Hong Kong through Colorcraft Ltd

10 9 8 7 6 5 4 3 2

contents

1 introduction—a guide for beginners 7
The reason for this book 7
Where can I find these natural materials? 8

2 natural materials 9
Leaves 9
Palms and palm-like plants 24
Shrubs 27
Trees 33
Vines and creepers 37

3 techniques to get you started 45
Under and over weaving—weave a table mat 46
Start a sculptural piece 46
Circular woven wall piece 48
Braiding or plaiting with three strands 53
Basic melon basket construction 54
Coiling a basket with easy random stitching 56

4 dyeing natural materials simply 59

5 projects you will find easy and fun 67
Happy harvest dolls 67
Wrap a tassel 68
Lavender wands 69
Three palm sheath containers 71
Plaited and sewn autumn mat 72
Stitched and coiled basket from the garden 73
Making a god's eye 74

Other useful materials 75
References 77
Index 78

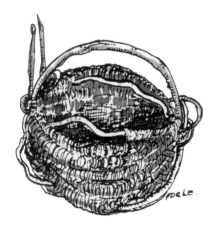

1 introduction—a guide for beginners

'Nearly everyone gains an infinite satisfaction and a happy glow of achievement from creating an object of value and charm from unpromising beginnings.'

Making use of common vegetable fibre gives one an inner glow of satisfaction and a very real sense of achievement, as if something in our ancestry has been brought to life—the basic need to be an individual in this modern mass produced society, but most of all the need to be a creative individual.

To be able to collect natural materials as found in gardens, fields and forests, make use of these fibres, the thrill of achievement, the discovery of one's creative ability, are the warmest, nicest feelings I know.

I think it was Ed Rossbach who made the comment about 'the drama of the process'. I teach to communicate the basketry experience, to have people feel the drama being played in their own hands; when the curtain closes on the finished basket, I delight in the joy they experience and their newfound awareness. From garden vines and prunings, they have, with time, allowed themselves this day.

THE REASON FOR THIS BOOK

This book is intended for the beginner and the student. Information has been kept simple so that you may be able to identify plant material and also so that you can develop your own traditions and uses for natural materials—the gathering, the preparation and the making. Many students in my classes and people I have spoken to at exhibitions and craft shows ask, 'How do I know what to collect and where do I find it?' As many people cannot identify even common garden plants, I have kept my plant descriptions to simple everyday terms and included an illustration of nearly every plant. Please do ask a neighbour (one with a nice garden). They are bound to help you with names and probably with material at pruning time.

Please do not gather materials in protected areas without obtaining a permit first.

I have also kept the techniques simple, so that you will develop your own as the construction problems arise. I have always seen my work as a problem solving exercise;

over the years, as I gained more experience with making, I became better at solving them.

At this point in our history I read about the time when basketry was produced for local village use—traditional baskets for everyday use, basketry for shelter, masks, fences, ceremonial objects and more. I also read of the changes made to village basketry by the demands from the outside world, for baskets mass produced like machine made products. People in China and the Philippines were trained to make maybe only one type of basket, so that is what they produced and of course became very very good at making a perfect little product one after the other. Please do not expect this standard of yourself, just enjoy the first attempts at working with the natural materials you have collected and prepared.

My intention is to encourage individual creativity, hoping that each person will feel a pride and warmth in this discovery—'Making for creativity's sake'.

WHERE CAN I FIND THESE NATURAL MATERIALS?

My town and its material sources

It is a good idea to write down your sources of local materials so that you can return to harvest something when suitable.

I live in the Strzelecki ranges of South Gippsland, the southernmost area of Victoria, Australia. It is an area well known for its rainfall, with undulating hills and creeks in between and at times an abundance of water in swamps, dams and drains. My house is on a block of 2.5 hectares on one of these hills and looks over the town of Leongatha and towards the distant ranges. It is surrounded by a large garden, in which I cultivate some of my basketry materials. Some of these plants include *Lomandra longifolia*, red-hot poker, irises, vines such as clematis, kennedia, passionfruit, jasmine and choko, wattle shrubs, cordyline, ferns, aralias, grasses, kangaroo paws and Allocasuarina shrubs or she-oaks.

There is always plenty of roadside material to harvest in the form of wild willows (several varieties), and the imported *Typha* or bulrush (now considered a weed), wild prunus (plums), apples and prickly hawthorn (I only use the new sucker-like growth that comes after it's cut back). The local council workers 'oblige' me by cutting back severely at times, thus providing new material one to two years later.

Many roadside grasses are weeds. Identify these and cut bundles before seed is formed. Take home and dry. If you take grasses with seeds attached, store where the mice cannot reach it.

My neighbours are a very important source of supply also and I am often invited into their gardens to prune and harvest, or receive a phone call to come and collect material before it goes to the tip. I am always careful to clip and cut only where invited, so that I may be invited back again.

The local farmers are also more than happy to have me prune their invasive river willows and cumbungi. This source of supply is very useful when I have a class to run and need large supplies suddenly.

I live in a city unit! I live in a very dry area!

Corn is the answer here. If you buy fresh corn on the cob to eat, save the outer husks, dry them in the sun, and store them in a paper bag until you have enough to use. You can also ask your local greengrocer or supermarket, 'What do you do with your stale corn?' Ask them to save some of the husks or sheaths for you. Let your friends know you want them—you will be surprised at just how willing they are to help. But don't forget to call and collect your treasure or they will not be too willing to save them again.

Also try walking. I have collected beautiful palm sheaths and fruiting stems, cordyline leaves and Philodendron sheaths from the most central part of Sydney, Australia's largest city. Take a walk through city parks and beach fronts; always carry a small pair of clippers and a plastic bag. It will be full in no time—most of what you will need is on the ground.

Back lanes and creeper covered fences are another source. Most people will be very happy for you to clip their overgrown ivy; just knock on the door and ask. And the best time of all is when the council has its regular garden garbage collection day. (Does this happen in your city?) All sorts of treasures are put out on the front nature strips. This is often your chance to collect some New Zealand flax leaves. Take nice long lengths suitable to sew or coil with (after you have dried them of course).

It is surprising just what can be found in dry areas—palms, grasses, grape vines, garden plants. Look through the Natural Materials section (pages 9–58) and always ask your neighbours.

Ask a florist. What they throw away may well be useful to you.

The plants included in this book are but a few in the world of plants. Some are suited to basketry techniques, many more are suitable for manipulation in some way to make a useful or decorative article. In fact as you become more used to working with natural materials and your awareness develops you may come to believe, as I do, that most plants have a use at some stage in their lives; it may be their roots, stems or leaves, flowers or fibre.

2 natural materials

To keep this book down to a manageable size, I have included only a few of the natural materials available. Some of the plants may not be known or available to everyone. Have fun and explore the possibilities of the plants you can recognise and collect.

Read the information on the various types of plant material and you will gradually understand how useful each one can be. New Zealand flax can even be used for tying up your garden plants after stripping. It is one of the very strong plant fibres.

If you still have difficulty identifying plants, look at some plant books, even ask at your local plant nursery. They may be able to show you a plant growing.

When it comes to preparing your materials do not get stressed out about the right and wrong way. There really is none. You will discover a new awareness and understanding of the different plants, the more you get to know their families and the more you explore their uses.

Follow the hints and clues I have given you with each plant. Look at other books on basketry. Test the flexibility of each plant material, twisting and wrapping leaves around your finger. If it is flexible when fresh or green, then it will certainly make a very pliable fibrous material when dried. Try leaves when they are dying, especially after a shower of rain. You should be able to tie knots in them. Bend vines into loops. Try the fresh shoots and the older material and try them at different times of the year. Be aware that some are great when fresh and some are only useable when dried and dampened.

But please—at all times obtain permission to collect your materials from nature reserves and private gardens.

LEAVES

Agave (*Agave americana*), Century plant (*Agave sisalana*)
FAMILY AGAVACEAE

Description This plant has gone wild in some places. It is easily recognised as the huge pointed leaf cactus that we see clumped around old building sites, or on dry roadside banks. It is a perennial succulent with sword-shaped, toothed leaves which form a basal rosette. It may be variegated or blue-green in colour. This large species

Agave

takes from 20 to 40 years to flower. The massive flowerspike bears bell-shaped, pale cream flowers and then the plant dies, leaving offsets which grow into new plants.

Agave sisalana is the source of the fibre sisal and the source of tequila, the Mexican national drink. The natural habitat of agave species is the arid or semi-arid tropics. They originated in Central America and are mostly grown commercially for their fibre in the tropics of America and Africa. It is grown in areas of South-East Asia and used for ropes and weft materials.

To harvest The fibre found in this plant's very large leaf, up to 1.5 m (5'), is very strong. To extract it, I was told that the natives of its country of origin break off the spike at the tip of the leaf, cut three-quarters of the way through the base of the leaf and then pull the spike downwards. I have done this and certainly extracted about 24 strands of fibre attached to the spike, making it a ready made needle and thread. There is a great amount of fibre still in the leaf after this; I have found removing it a very slow process, but it is possible, by beating the fleshy leaf with a flat board. This helps it to dry. The material can be roughly combed into lengths with a comb made with nails driven into a strip of wood. The lengths of fibre are then tied into loose bundles, washed and hung in coils to dry.

Another method is to soak the leaf in warm water or even boil it (you will probably need a very large pot). Keep the plant material covered and warm and the flesh rots. You can scrape this away and fine fibres can be extracted. This may be more useful for paper makers and people who spin.

To use Slightly dampen before use. It is a hard strong fibre such as we know in sisal rope. It may be used for sewing, weaving, coiling and spinning into cordage.

Availability Widespread, in gardens and along roadsides.

Arum Lily, Common White Lily (*Zantedeschia aethiopica*)
FAMILY ARACEAE

Description This large white lily originates in South Africa. It is very hardy and is commonly found in old gardens and moist spots. Its long stems are thick and very succulent with a large, shiny, triangular shaped leaf at the tip. The white lily flower grows from the clump on its own stem about 2 cm (^{3}/4") in diameter, and can be over 1 m (40") tall. The cone shaped flower is thick, with a stiff yellow spadix coming from the centre. In moist climates it can stay evergreen.

To harvest Cut stems of leaves and flowers in summer and hang to dry in a warm spot. They may take eight weeks to dry in some climates. They will shrink away to a fraction of their original size. You may find a plant that has dried off in summer and is easily pulled away stem by stem from the clump. Tie into bundles and store for later use.

To use This material when dampened (just enough to soften) is beautiful to work with. It has length and is strong and satiny. Good for weaving, plaiting and tying.

Availability Gardens; a roadside weed in some areas where it has naturalised.

Bulrush, Cattail, Cumbungi, Lesser reed-mace (*Typha domingensis, T. orientalis, T. latifolia*)
FAMILY TYPHACEAE

Description The old English name for what we call cumbungi (*Typha*) in Australia was 'poolrush' which later became 'bulrush'.

This plant grows in watery places, such as dams, drains, swamps, rivers, creeks or gutters. It is a large aquatic plant with long strap-like leaves growing from rhizomes (underground stems) by which the plant spreads. The flowers are at the top of an upright stem.

There are three known species, *Typha domingensis* and *T. orientalis* being indigenous, while *T. latifolia* was introduced to Australia. *T. domingensis* likes fresh water and ponds and *T. orientalis* is known to live in salt water. The main distinguishing feature is the flower head. *T. domingensis* has dense cylindrical spikes on tall stems above the foliage. Male clusters are 20–50 mm above the female flowers. The spikes of the other two species are smaller. In *T. latifolia*, a serious weed, the spikes are dark chocolate pokers, very different from the paler tan poker flowers of the native species, and in winter the plant becomes dormant.

To harvest Material from these plants is best collected when in peak growing condition in all areas, and before frosts cause damage. You will need to take a long carving knife to cut the butts of the rush as far under the water as possible, as it is this butt end that provides some of the best material. It is better to collect the rush when there is water still near the butts, not when they are high on a dry bank for example, or they may dry hard and brittle instead of soft and satiny. They can also become hard if left to dry in the hot summer sun.

Arum lily

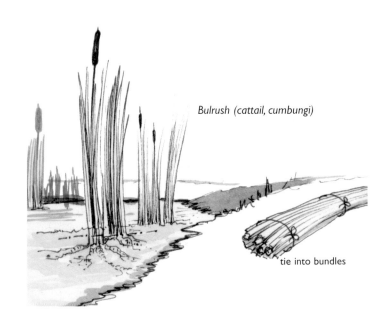

Bulrush (cattail, cumbungi)

tie into bundles

Tie the cut bundles of rush together in about three places, so that they do not bend or crack. I find that after leaving these bundles in a shady dry place, for about a week, the leaves will separate from the clump with little effort. At this stage you may separate all the stems, wipe them free of the jelly-like substance that is contained in the butt end, sort them into sizes and tie into bundles again in three places and dry them in a dark, dry, shady and airy place (e.g. in an old shed, under the house or the carport) for about six weeks. Hanging from the top end is ideal.

To store After 4–6 weeks drying the rushes may be taken down; if they are soft enough to bend, you can pack them into a long cardboard box. Otherwise, if they are stiffish, roll bundles together in thick newsprint tied in two or three places. As long as it is kept dry, this material will last for years.

To use When you are ready to use the material, the rushes must be dampened. Immerse them in water (the bath is the best place to do this) for one or two hours and then wrap in a damp towel overnight. Or hose them on the lawn and cover with damp hessian bags and leave overnight. Wipe the rushes clean with a damp towel and trim butt ends, preparing enough for a day's work. Do not make them too moist as there will be a large amount of shrinkage and the work may be loose when finished.

This material is excellent and most satisfying to work with. The butt ends are usually used as stake material, being the strongest. The weaving material is usually the upper part of the rush, and the twining or pairing weave (page 47) is the most suitable technique. Check weave or over and under weaving with the butt end is also excellent, making sure that all stakes are the same width. Rushes may also be plaited and coiled and used for sewing; they are also used for rush seating. Projects such as Happy Harvest Dolls (page 67) can be made from the spare rush.

Availability Widespread on creeks and river banks, lagoons, lakes, farm dams and swampy ground and drains. Most farmers would be happy to let you cut the rushes on their land, especially on the irrigation properties, as rushes have become a pest in many areas.

Cane grass (*Eragrostis australasica*)
FAMILY POACEAE

Description This Australian native is a handsome clumping plant, found growing in swampy or part swampy ground, often in association with lignum. After rain it produces new growth of long slender canes amongst the old dead pieces. The leaves are attached to nodes on the canes, but they hug the stem closely, like bamboo. Stems can be 2–5 m (6'–16') tall.

To harvest To dry for later use, twist the fresh canes into coils and allow to shrink or dry before weaving over them.

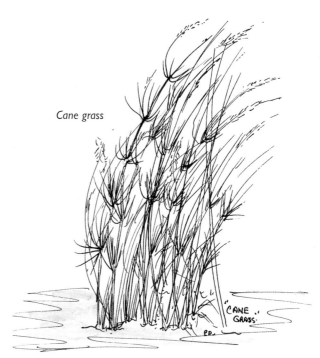

Cane grass

To use Because of the length of this material you can twist the canes into coils quite easily. They dry quite rigid and are suitable for framework, e.g. melon basket technique and wreaths.

Availability Cane grass is fairly common in claypans and shallow and dry swamps in the drier areas of most states.

Canna lily (*Canna* spp.)
FAMILY CANNACEAE

Description Robust, showy, rhizomatous perennials, these plants are at their best in late summer. They die off in winter. The tall cannas with cane-like stems have large tropical looking leaves and large clusters of cream, orange, pink, red or yellow flowers. They have been popular in parks and gardens where they are planted in massed beds. I have found the tall red leaved form the best to use as it retains a good colour. They can be grown by division of the rhizomes.

To harvest Collect the leaves with their stems attached. Flowering stems may be useful also. Some of the dead material around clumps may be useful, but most plants can be cut before winter, when the plant will die down.

To store Pull leaves off stems and pack them in boxes or large paper bags; stems can be tied in bundles for possible use.

To use As there is a lot of moisture in these plants, the stems will take up more moisture than needed if left in water too long, so dipping in water for one or two minutes is sufficient. Then wrap in a damp towel before use.

The stems, although short, make very fine weaving material, and can be twined and used for stakes. Their

Canna lily

dark colour provides a fine contrast with lighter coloured material.

The leaves are very wide and can be used to line a basket, laying them flat and stitching in place. They may also be coiled, twisted, plaited and woven.

Availability In public gardens and becoming popular in home gardens as well. Can sometimes be found growing on roadsides where garden rubbish has been dumped.

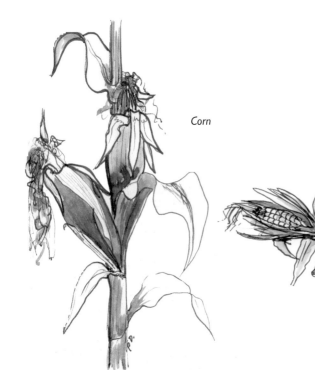
Corn

Corn (*Zea mays*)
FAMILY POACEAE

Description An annual crop and vegetable plant, corn grows up to 2 m (6') high, producing male and female flowers separately. The male inflorescences or tassels are terminal and the female flowers or ears are lateral, enclosed by numerous husks (modified leaves). The silks are the long stigmas of the female flowers. The fruit or kernels, which may be variously coloured, adhere to the cob.

Corn husks were used by the Native Americans to make dolls. They taught this craft to the early European settlers in that country.

To harvest
Husks When corn is mature on the cob, you will be able to collect nice large husks (the wrappings around the corn). Separate each husk, tie them together in loose bundles and store to dry. Drying time approximately six weeks.
Leaves Pick the largest and longest leaves, when cobs of corn are finishing. Collect only the best leaves, and tie them in bundles and store in large brown paper bags to dry.
Silks The silks attached to the cob may be used to make hair, e.g. for corn dolls.
Cobs There are various types of corn. One particular variety, that is not very edible but is very decorative, is the Squaw Corn. The cobs are very colourful and you never know what colour you have until you remove the husks at maturity. A special corn was developed about 1946 in Missouri in the United States which grows a hardwood cob, twice the length of regular corn cobs, for corn cob pipes. This variety has a small white kernel.

To use
Husks Soak husks in warm water for five minutes or until pliable. You must always work with husks wet. Wrap excess in a damp towel until ready for use. The husks may be split and plaited, used flat as for corn husk dolls, or twisted and coiled as in the coiled basketry techniques. Corn husks also take dye very well.
Leaves Prepare for use as for husks. Leaves may be split into 1–1.5 cm ($^3/_8$"–$^1/_2$") strips and plaited into a continuous length, or they may be twisted for use in coil

baskets. The centre veins left after the leaves have been stripped of soft material for plaiting may be used as foundation stakes for the base of a small basket.

Silks The silks are first dried. For use soak for 5 minutes and then use in a slightly damp condition to make braided hair or wrapped around the head in a desired hair style. This is then stitched in place.

The above materials, husks, leaves and silks, can all be dyed before use.

Cobs Dried cobs may be cut through the centre or sliced into slabs with a small handsaw and used kernel side up, or centre up, glued into designs for wall plaques.

The cobs for corn cob pipes are stripped of the kernels and aged for about two years, before being crafted on a lathe into bowls for the pipes, to which bamboo stems are added. Originally this stem was a reed.

Availability Corn is a popular garden vegetable and can be purchased in most supermarkets with the husks intact (eat the corn and dry the husks).

Cymbidium (Orchid) (*Cymbidium* spp.)
FAMILY ORCHIDACEAE

Description Many people grow the orchids of this species in pots, and they can be very hardy, even outdoors in southern Australia. Growers repot and divide up clumps of bulbs and trim off the very tough and long leaves.

To harvest Collect the leaves when repotting the plants. You can dry before storing them by leaving them for about ten days in a dry shady spot. You must allow for shrinkage. When fresh you can split the leaves in quarters lengthwise to weave or plait with. They are very strong and a good length to use for stitching, coiling and wrapping.

To use Dampen and leave overnight in a damp towel. Weave or plait. This is strong material when fresh and can be used for tying.

Availability Any grower will gladly save you some leaves when the plants are being thinned out, just ask your friends to spread the word.

Day lily (*Hemerocallis fulva*)
FAMILY LILIACEAE

Description This popular, hardy, garden plant has mostly yellow or orange flowers, but some varieties have white, red or purple. Day lilies form clumps and are perennials. Some types are dormant in winter. Some have long, fibrous, sword-like leaves to about 90 cm (36") and some have shorter leaves. It is the longer-leafed type that is more useful, if you have a choice of plants. The flowers are borne in succession, each one lasting for about a day. It is one of my favourite plants.

To harvest I collect from my plants when the outside leaves are at their longest, pulling them away from the bottom of the clump during their growing season, and collecting the remains of the clump when the plant is moving into its dormant period, when leaves start to yellow and dry out. They do retain a better colour at this stage. Hang them to dry as for red-hot poker leaves (page 22).

To use Day lily leaves are thin and do not need a long soak, no more than ten minutes; dip in water and wrap in a damp towel until pliable. These leaves are strong and can be used for weaving, plaiting, stitching, coiling and cordage. They can be twisted with the finer leaves.

Cymbidium

Day lily

Popular as a garden plant; older style gardens may have large clumps of them. In America *Hemerocallis fulva* has escaped and become semi-wild on roadsides and other areas.

Dianella—Native flax or Flax lily, Tasman flax lily, Blueberry (*Dianella tasmanica*)
Spreading flax lily (*D. revoluta*)
Paroo lily (*D. caerulea*)
Smooth flax lily (*D. laevis, syn. D. longifolia*)
FAMILY LILIACEAE

Description The strong upright leaves of dianella can be up to 1 m (40") long with variations depending on the species and the growing conditions.

In my garden they will stand very dry conditions, but for use in basketry, I grow them in shade and let them form large clumps to force the leaves up to the light, giving the maximum length. They are attractive plants which will spread around the garden, giving you pleasure when they flower and later producing the most wonderful blue berries.

To harvest Pull or cut the leaves as close to the ground as possible, and leave them to stand in a tall cardboard box to dry, or strip them into finer strands (I use a meat skewer for this). Twist this fine material into coils and dry them in a box or paper bag. You can also dry them flat, by rolling them around a cardboard tube and holding them with paper clips, or tape them to newspaper and press them under a large floor rug. They dry a very nice grey-green or light brown.

To use You will need to soak the leaves for an hour in cold or warm water, then wrap them in a damp towel, best overnight as they are a strong fibrous material and will not work well for you if they are dry. You can use this material in many ways as the strong fibre will allow you to plait, weave or make twine. It is also ideal for coiling and stitching. When partly dry you could use it as ties for a bush shelter or similar construction.

Availability People who have native gardens will gladly let you have some of this plant, but the best way is to grow it in your own backyard. Most Australian native plant nurseries will have a plants available.

Ginger plant, Ginger lily (*Hedychium gardnerianum*)
FAMILY ZINGIBERACEAE

Description This plant has a similar growth habit to the canna lily—long slender stems, fleshy, with longish leaves. It has heads of yellow and red scented flowers. The plants grow in a clump from a rhizome and can be quite tall in good conditions, rich soil well watered.

To harvest Stems can be cut at ground level when the flower has dried. Leave to dry in a shady spot. I have cut mine and tossed them under a dry shady tree in summer and they dry in good condition. They can take a little longer than some leaves to dry out completely, as their stems are full of moisture. Store them rolled in newspaper until required.

To use When dry, the leaves pull away from the main stems easily. You will have a leaf with stem attached which I find excellent weaving or coiling material. Use the main stem also. They require very little dampening. A quick dunking and wrapping in a towel is sufficient. This material is soft to use and can be plaited if a rustic look

Dianella tasmanica

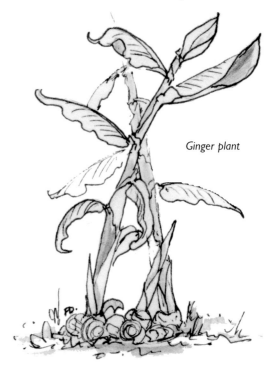

Ginger plant

is required and you have a large quantity. You could then stitch the plait into a basket. I like to twine them into a twig basket to add texture.

Availability Hardy and grown in many gardens, often becoming a very large clump, so neighbours would gladly have you cut some, if you ask.

Gladiolus (*Gladiolus* spp.)
FAMILY IRIDACEAE

Description Gladioli are very popular garden plants which grow from underground corms. They produce spikes of funnel-shaped flowers with erect, sword-shaped leaves at the base of the flower stems.

To harvest To ensure the corm will flower the next year, it is important not to harvest the leaves until the plant has died down. Remove leaves from the main flowering stem. They can be stored tied in bundles in large brown paper bags, making sure they are quite dry before storing away as mildew will soon spoil them. Drying may take 4–6 weeks. Check the stored leaves from time to time, as they are very prone to mould attack, and keep them moving about.

To use Soak leaves in water for ten minutes, then wrap in a towel. This is a fairly strong material, the leaves containing a lot of fibre, so that it can be twisted, plaited, twined, coiled and woven.

Availability Gardens or bulb farms. I used to collect leaves from a local bulb farm. When the bulbs are lifted the tops are in very good condition and the grower will not want them. Gardeners who grow them will happily save the leaves for you when they want to lift the corms.

Iris, Common flag (*Iris germanica, I. sibirica, I. spuria*)
FAMILY IRIDACEAE

Description This popular and well known garden flower comes from a vast family of plants, some of which grow from bulbs, some from rhizomes. It is the latter that we want. Plants grown on rhizomes make excellent border plants forming clumps. The long slender leaves of some irises make superior basketry material when dried.. This is a very fibrous strong material. Look for the longest leaves which can measure up to 1 m (40"). The plant dies down each winter. Leaves from the bulbous irises can also be used, but generally they are not available in such quantity. Collect leaves from any iris varieties you have access to.

To harvest Pull leaves from plant when still in good condition but after flowering. I harvest from the outside of the clump, pulling off the longest leaves and leaving the shorter leaves to grow on. Dry them in shade in a dry airy place as they are very prone to mildew attack, tie and twist into bundles and store in a cardboard box for later use. Can give excellent colour in the off-white to pale yellow range.

To use Dampen bundle in water for perhaps five minutes, then wrap in a damp towel. I use these leaves for twining, twisting into ropes for melon baskets, coiling, stitching and wrapping. A wonderful fibre to work with. I just love it when my neighbours ask me to come and prune their iris clumps.

Availability Very common garden plant; sometimes found semi-wild surviving in paddocks in some areas, sometimes in old cemeteries and home sites. Many varieties need garden conditions to survive.

Gladiolus

Iris sibirica

Kaffir lily (*Clivia miniata*)
FAMILY AMARYLLIDACEAE

Description Commonly found in old gardens, the kaffir lily is easy to grow from a piece of an old clump. Kaffir lilies have strap-like dark green leaves with salmon-orange flowers in clusters.

To harvest These leaves may be collected all year round. The stems of the flowers can also be collected, either green, when they may take up to three months to dry completely, or in their dying state straight from the plant, when they may dry in half the time. The leaves become very thin when dry and the butt also dries out thin.

To use Wrap in a damp towel or leave out on a damp night. This material needs only a little moisture to make it supple again, so do not soak it, oherwise there will be too much swelling, resulting in a lot of shrinkage. The flower stem, although short, needs a slightly longer soaking as it is thicker.
   This material remains a very nice golden colour and could be used to feature when colour is needed. It also plaits and twists well, and may be used in coiled and twined work.

Availability Gardens. An old fashioned plant found usually in border plantings under large trees. Survives neglect.

Kaffir lily (Clivea miniata)

Kangaroo paws—Yellow kangaroo paw (*Anigozanthos flavidus*), Red-green kangaroo paw (*A. manglesii*)
FAMILY HAEMODORACEAE

Description Evergreen perennials with thick rootstocks and sword-shaped leaves, kangaroo paws have unusual bird-attracting flowers. The tall form of *A. flavidus* can grow flower stalks up to 3 m (10') long. The leaves are interesting to use; the longer they grow the easier they are

Yellow kangaroo paw

to work with. They can be over 1 m (40") in length. Flower stems may be of use for some projects as they are long lasting and rigid. The plants grow best in a dry airy position, preferably dry throughout the growing season as they are prone to spotting.

To harvest You may pluck the leaves from a healthy plant when in good growing condition, or when a large clump is to be divided. They will dry to an unusual silver green or grey green and will take 4–6 weeks to dry. Tie in bundles when dry and store.

To use Soak leaves in cold water about five minutes, wrap in a towel and leave for a few hours. They should be strong and leathery. They may be woven or can be coiled and twisted. Nice combined with another plant for colour variation.

Availability These Western Australian plants are very common in gardens around the world these days.

Mat rush, Spiny-headed (*Lomandra longifolia*)
FAMILY XANTHORRHOAECEAE

Description This large clumping plant has leaves over 1 m (40") long, with flowers borne on long flat-sided stems. I have had one growing in my garden for about fifteen years, during which time I have harvested the leaves whenever the plant needs a good cutting back. I have usually chopped into it, rather than cut, as the leaves are so long. It grows on a well drained bank and

Happy harvest dolls made from bulrush. This shows the use of the butt end of the rush (page 67)

NATURAL MATERIALS

Willow prunings suitable for stake material (page 36)

Basketry materials from my collection—twisted circles of vines, dried leaves and grasses, fruits, palm sheath and palm stems

NATURAL MATERIALS

Day lily

Background: pale rush flowers

Trunk of paperbark

New Zealand flax

Bulrush (cumbungi)

Flowers of native hibiscus—good for dyeing

19

Bulrush weaving with wisteria handle

Wild willow used for both stakes and weavers

overhangs a pathway and each year it happily replaces the cut area. The flower stems can also be useful.

Lomandra multiflora was used on the west coast of Cape York Peninsula by the Wik Mungkan people who made a string from the plant to fashion soft baskets, using a twined technique.

To harvest Leaves may be plucked or pulled from the plant. Generally only leaves of a certain size will come away, a method used by the southern Australian Aboriginals to collect leaves of a regular size. These would then be left to dry a little in the bush, or split and pulled through hot ashes to soften and make them pliable. Or you can cut leaves near the base and partly dry them for use. Flower stems may also be cut. This material is stiff and dries to a very nice pale straw colour. Tie it into bundles in 2–3 places (as it will crack). You may split the leaves down their length if wanted for core material and store in bundles; most of the shrinkage will have taken place in the first 2–3 weeks, but it will take a total of 5–6 weeks to dry completely. Tie the flower stems separately.

To use I find I can use this material when it is partly dry. It makes excellent stakes or uprights, as do the flower stems. It may need a long soaking if dried completely, e.g. half an hour in water then overnight wrapped in a damp towel. It can be split and used for core material in stitched and coiled basketry and also as the wrapping on coiled work. It is strong enough for weaving.

Availability Gardens; it is still found growing in its natural state in many areas around Australia. It has become a common plant in streetscape plantings of recent times, and I am sure you would be able to collect some when council gardeners are cutting back clumps. There are long forms, e.g. *L. longifolia*, and shorter forms.

Mat rush

New Zealand flax (*Phormium tenax*)
Family Agavaceae

Description New Zealand flax plants can vary in colour, being dark or light green, variegated or bronze, and may be stiff and upright or quite bent over. The New Zealand Maoris preferred a dark green form. The broad leaves can be fine, strong, up to 3 cm (1^1/$_4$") wide and about 70 cm (28") long. The clump is made up of many 'hands', so a hand may be cut away to start a new plant.

The flower stems and seed heads are longer than the leaves when mature, and are weighed down by their heavy seed heads to such an extent that the head hangs in the dirt. The plant will have many of these stems and if you gently run your hand down a bundle of the leaves, the flower stems or seed head will come away in your hand, with very little pressure. They are good for dried flower arrangements.

To harvest Collect healthy leaves. Select for long length and cut low at the butt end. Never cut the central shoot or the next pair of leaves, thus ensuring the plant is left with enough leaves to continue growing.

To use Split off the back rib as there is no useful fibre in it. Cut off the butt end and coloured edges of the leaf (illustrations A and B on next page). Split remaining leaf in half, then into quarters (illustration C), and double (you now have 8 lengths). These can be 'stressed' by running each strip across a sharp corner such as the edge of a bench. Hold firmly and do this two or three times. You may use them now for flat weaving or plaiting or you can roll the strips into a coil, adding one at a time until you have a solid coil which will store flat and can be used when a little shrinkage has taken place, about 3–4 weeks depending on weather conditions. Tie with flax edge.

Your next choice is to further strip the sections very finely with a fine point, e.g. needle or meat skewer (see the project Wrap a Tassel on page 68). Twist this material into small coils about 15 cm (6") in diameter to store after boiling. To boil pop into a pan of water and boil 2–3 minutes. Then dry by threading a length of flax (from edge) through six coils and hanging them in a tree. Store in an old pillowcase or cardboard box. You can store your flax for years by doing this.

Flax prepared this way is dampened for re-use (place in warm water for few minutes until you can feel it soften). You can use it as a core for a coiled and stitched basket, for very fine twined work, you can sew with it, or use it for sculptured work where a mass of soft fibre is needed. It is a strong fibre and will stand a lot of handling.

Note Do not overwet New Zealand flax as the wetter it is the more it shrinks as it dries; your weaving or work will open up and look loose.

Availability Popular garden plant and very hardy. Used around Australia in parks and street planting and available in many countries. Also try your local rubbish collection or tip. Ask your neighbour.

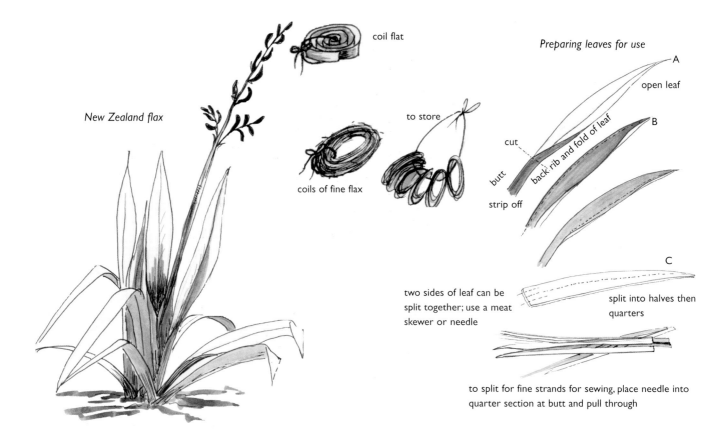

New Zealand flax

coil flat

to store

coils of fine flax

Preparing leaves for use

A

open leaf

B

cut

butt

back rib and fold of leaf

strip off

C

two sides of leaf can be split together; use a meat skewer or needle

split into halves then quarters

to split for fine strands for sewing, place needle into quarter section at butt and pull through

Red-hot poker (*Kniphofia* spp.)
FAMILY LILIACEAE OR ALOEACEAE

Description This popular garden plant has long strappy leaves with long-stemmed poker flowers ranging from red to yellow. There are many varieties whose leaves vary in length from 40 to 150 cm (16"–60"). It is a perennial clumping plant; some are evergreen.

Red-hot poker

To harvest Collect the longest leaves from healthy plants by pulling or cutting them at the base of the clump. I like to tie them together by the tips and hang them to dry for about six weeks in a dry airy place. Make sure you tie the tips together and then fold them over and tie again. This saves you having to pick leaves off the floor as they shrink when drying and slip out. When dry twist them into coils and store for later use in a box. Some basket-makers dry their leaves in newspaper. This may suit your situation. Just lay the leaves on sheets of paper and roll them up, but check them constantly as they can be attacked by mildew. Change the newspaper frequently.

To use Soak these leaves for about ten minutes in water and then wrap in a towel until they are soft and pliable. This will not take long. This material is strong and soft and can be used for weaving, stitching, plaiting and tying. I find it excellent.

Availability Many gardens will have one of these plants and neighbours will gladly give you leaves, especially in autumn. Some areas may have it growing along the roadsides and on old home sites.

Pale Rush (*Juncus pallidus*)
FAMILY JUNCACEAE

Description A large rush with a tall, firm stem which can be 1–2 m high. The Juncas family has pith inside the stems.

Pale rush (Juncus spp.)

To harvest These stems need to be collected with care as the longer types are quite liable to break if bent. Harvest by pulling from the base of the plant or cutting. Tie into bundles top and bottom. Some types have a nice brown colouring at the base of the plant which you may desire to use in the edges of your work.

To use

Method 1 Prepare to use by soaking in warm water in a bath, then wrap in a damp towel until ready to use. The stems can take some time to become pliable so test before you use them by wrapping around your hand. If they will bend without cracking then they are ready.

Method 2 This method was demonstrated to me by an Aboriginal craftswoman. Pluck the rushes and while fresh use your fingernail or a large darning needle to stick through the stem and run it through from tip to butt, opening up the rush so that you can see the pithy matter inside; remove this with your thumbnail by pushing it up from the bottom. The soft outside part is ready to use when dried and dampened. It will dry quickly to a pleasant shade and is ideal for coil techniques and weaving.

Availability Found in wettish places, these plants were once the enemy of the farmer in low-lying farming areas. They had to dig out the 'tussocks', as they are called, year after year as they are very determined survivors. I have these plants growing successfully in my garden on a hill. Look along river and creek banks and drains; they can be quite prolific in some areas.

Tall leaf rush (*Cyperus lucidus*), Papyrus (*C. papyrus*)
FAMILY CYPERACEAE

Description Although sharp on the edges, the leaves of these rushes can be cut at the butt end, and once they start to dry they can be handled quite well. Leaves split straight with a sharp point like a needle, and can be used in twining or cordage and plaiting. Very nice to work with after two days drying.

Flower stems are large strong three-sided stems with a papyrus-like flowerhead of dark brown. Stems dry to a very attractive colour.

Papyrus comes from Egypt and is well known as the plant that the Egyptian 'paper' was made from; it came to fame again in recent times when the stems were used by Thor Heyerdahl to make the raft *Kon-Tiki*.

This tall plant with umbrella-like fronds can grow to 6 m (20') in its native habitat on the upper Nile River. However, in most garden situations it grows to only about one-third of that. The thick stems are three-sided and thick at the base, very firm and strong, standing

Papyrus

upright, and tapering near the top where short fronds fan out.

To harvest Stems can be cut at ground level and dried. The stem has a firm outer skin with a soft pithy material inside. The fronds can also be used.

To use I found I could cut the stem into strips, and use them for weaving once dampened. The tassel-like fronds can also be put to use as hair for harvest dolls or simply used as the core for a coiled basket.

Availability Gardens; this plant has been popular for many years as a feature plant around rockeries and ponds.

PALMS AND PALM-LIKE PLANTS

Alexandra palm (*Archontophoenix alexandrae*)
FAMILY ARECACEAE

Description A tall slender palm, the Alexandra palm can reach 15–25 m. The trunk is marked with rings from fallen leaves or fronds. The branched fronds form a crown of feather-shaped leaves 2–3 m (6'–10') long. It produces sprays of small white flowers in autumn.

To harvest
Leaves I have collected three or four of the discarded leaves, that is, the crown shaft and leaf stalk, annually for the past five years from a palm growing in my garden. Collect the leaflets green, and dry to store. The crown shaft is best manipulated into a shape soon after falling from the palm. It can be cut and folded, as if making a box, and with a few large stitches kept in place.
Inflorescences When the fruit has dropped off these large, multi-branched panicles may be pulled off the tree (very easily), or collected from the ground.

To use The inflorescences provide wonderful texture and can be woven or coiled. Papery bracts encasing the inflorescence drop off before the flowers open. These may be torn into strips and used for weaving. Sometimes you may need to dampen the inflorescences a little before use. When dried, the crown shaft may be soaked and manipulated into shape or cut into strips and used for weaving. A good long soak overnight will make them pliable enough to fold and stitch into containers. See page 71.

Availability This palm grows naturally from Mackay in Queensland to Cape York, but is also grown around Sydney, and I have had one growing in a sheltered courtyard in southern Victoria for the past five years. It is sold through nurseries and supermarkets as an indoor plant, and is planted out in many sheltered gardens.

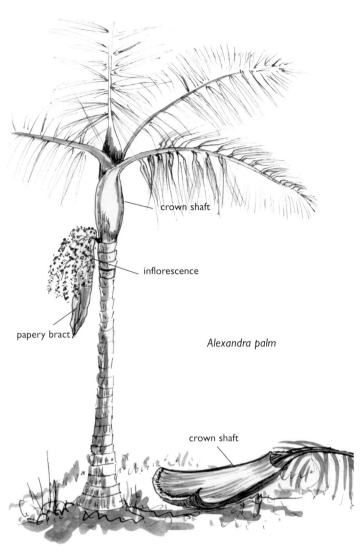

crown shaft

inflorescence

papery bract

Alexandra palm

crown shaft

Cabbage tree palm, Fan palm (*Livistonia australis*)
FAMILY ARECACEAE

Description This is the only palm native to the south-eastern part of the continent, growing from Queensland to Victoria; it is protected in its Victorian habitat in East Gippsland. It is a slow growing palm with a slender, grey trunk and fan-shaped leaves 1 m (40") across, divided into pointed glossy green leaflets. It produces long sprays of yellow flowers in spring. There are many varieties of fan-like palms in this genus which is found in Australia and South-East Asia. Try any of the fan palm family if you have access to them. A similar type of palm, the Lontar fan palm, is used in South-East Asia in a similar way.

The Aborigines in New South Wales used this plant to weave baskets, make fishing nets and make roofs for shelters. The tender young heart of the tree was used as food by both Aborigines and early European settlers, but harvesting it resulted in the death of the palm.

This is the palm known as the source of the cabbage tree hats worn by early settlers. There are examples of these in some of our museums and they are a very light coloured plaited hat, some of them very fine and quite beautiful.

To harvest The unopened newly formed leaf or branch was collected to make the cabbage tree hat. To prepare the leaf for hat making it is boiled, for half an hour to two hours, until the desired colour is achieved and the leaf has become finer. It can then be dried and stored for later use. It is split into thin even lengths from which a fine plait may be made that is both light in weight and colour when eventually stitched into a hat.

Young fronds can be cut and dried for the best material for other purposes. They are best collected at the partly opened or unopened stage. Do not cut all new growth or the plant may die. The best of the leaflets from fallen fronds may be collected and dried also. Strip the leaf along the fold and pull each segment from the stem to dry and store.

The women of Aurukun on Cape York Peninsula, and in northern and western Queensland, cut the unopened branch, pull it apart and strip the fibre from under the surface of each segment. The strips of fibre, up to 1.5 m (5') long and about 5 cm (2") wide, are dried in the sun for a few minutes before use.

The inflorescence may also be collected (see Alexandra palm, previous page).

To use Dampen fronds and wrap in a towel. This material can be woven, coiled or plaited; if split and rolled into string, it makes a fairly stiff string. Dampen the inflorescence for weaving or coiling. Palm frond can be dyed successfully (see page 59).

Availability Garden plant, fallen fronds in parks, may be naturalised in some countries.

Cordyline (*Cordyline australis*)
FAMILY AGAVACEAE

Description This very hardy New Zealand plant is not a true palm. Cordylines were very popular in the 1960s in Australia when rock and pebble gardens were the craze. It was often planted with New Zealand flax. Most people who have it growing near a lawn will be aware that the tough strap-like leaves can 'jam' the lawnmower if they get caught in it. It starts life as a small grassy-looking plant, eventually growing a trunk and becoming palm-like. Its dead leaves remain attached to the trunk for a long time. It will develop several 'tops' or heads, usually after flowering. The flowers are large fine bunches of white flowers. Still quite a common plant, it is very easy to grow even in a pot. Most people will gladly give you some leaves if you ask.

Cabbage tree palm or fan palm

Cordyline australis

To harvest Pull green leaves from the plants with the butt end attached if possible (although this can require extra strength). The dead leaves pull off more easily, but do not collect them if they are too tattered. Best collected from plants that have been grown well. The leaves from a plant growing in tough dry conditions will be very tough and difficult to work with.

To use I like to use these leaves when they are about three-quarters dry for some techniques; if you want to stitch and coil them, it is best to strip them finely, the full length of the leaf, then dry them and dampen when needed. When collected fresh the green leaves are very strong and fibrous, and may be stripped and used for string, tying and weaving. Very useful as stakes when bundled together.

Availability Cordylines have been a very popular and extremely hardy garden and tub plant. Common in older gardens, park and street plantings.

Pandanus (*Pandanus spiralis, P. aquaticus*)
FAMILY PANDANACEAE

Description A palm-like multi-branched tree; the leaves are at the ends of the branches and very fibrous. They are long and flat, tapered to the tip, with claw-like small spines along the edges and midrib.

To use Australian Aboriginal peoples prepare the leaves by first stripping the thorns from the sides and the midrib. This is done with two movements, holding the folded leaf and using the thumbnail. Then they strip each piece into two to three lengths and actually splice the leaf, i.e. separate the back layer of the leaf from the front layer (a technique that needs quite a lot of practice). Once this is done the remaining sections are split again to suit the user. The pile from one surface of the leaf is used as core material and from the other surface is used for the wrapping when making coiled baskets, after it has all been boiled and then dyed and dried. Pandanus is beautiful material to use when prepared this way and may be used for Aboriginal twined dilly bags or mats and ceremonial objects.

The tall stems become light (buoyant) and are hollow after falling and have been used for didgeridoos; in the past they were tied together to make rafts.

Aboriginal peoples in the Top End have used pandanus extensively; around Broome in Western Australia it was used to make footwear.

In Fiji the palm is woven flat and used for sleeping mats and eating mats. The women collect and dry the leaves, stripping off the thorns and flattening the leaf, pressing down on the rib. They then start to roll this leaf into a coil, adding many extra leaves, until it has reached a manageable size. This is then held together with a piece of leaf tied through the centre and across the end of the

last leaf. The coil is unwound and the leaves laid flat in the sun to dry, then the coiling procedure starts again. This is repeated with constant pushing and pressing of the leaves until the whole coil is dried to the weaver's satisfaction. It may be dyed black at this stage and, if not needed for weaving, will be sold at a market place.

A similar procedure is used in parts of Bali, Indonesia, with a smaller variety of pandanus. The leaves are coiled into octagonal shapes and used to weave mats as used in the temple to present offerings. You may come across the coils and mats set out to dry on the edge of the road as you drive around villages in the mornings. This material is used for flat plaiting or weaving.

Availability Many varieties grow in the warmer climates of the world and can be found in gardens.

Detail of pandanus leaf

thorny edge being stripped off
centre rib is also taken off

Pandanus

SHRUBS

Box thorn (*Lycium ferocissimum*)
FAMILY SOLANACEAE

Description A straggling, spiny shrub to 3 m (10"), with drooping branches and fleshy leaves growing in clusters on small shoots. The white to pale mauve flowers form in leaf axils, producing orange-red fruit.

To harvest Collect roots and strip the bark before the roots dry out. The roots and the outer bark may be used. Coil into bundles to dry. The supple stems can also be used, although the thorns can be a problem! I once found a seriously chopped-back bush that had put out an abundance of new, clean (no thorns) growth stems the previous season. I was able to collect many lengths or rods from this bush.

To use The stripped root is very pliable when green and can be used in this state. Root pieces can be tied into various shapes while green and then used for handles when dry. The stems are as supple as willow and can be used for melon or twig style baskets.

Availability This plant was introduced from South Africa to Australia for use as a hedge by early settlers on farms. It was proclaimed a noxious weed in the early 1900s. It has gone wild in many places, as the birds eat the berries and distribute the seeds. It occurs on dry land, along fence lines, scattered through paddocks and in irrigation channels, and on roadsides and in cemeteries.

Hibiscus, Native (*Alyogyne huegelii*)
FAMILY AMARANTHACEAE

Description This shrub has hairy branches and leaves, but the thing you notice most is its very showy large blue-purple (sometimes white, yellow or mauve) hibiscus-like flowers. It is a very vigorous grower under good conditions, and needs to be pruned back annually. The flowers give a rosy-purple dye (see Dyeing natural materials simply, page 59).

To harvest When you have cut back the plant, trim off the small branchlets close to the main stems. Now harvest the bark from the branches by making long straight cuts into the bottom end of the stem, and then lifting the bark away from the woody part, pulling upwards until you have taken all of the usable bark away. The bark is is very pliable. It can be split again to recover a fine fibre and inner bark by slipping a tool such as a meat skewer or strong needle between the outer and inner bark layers. Store by twisting into coils, dry if wanted for later use.

To use Soak until just soft—no longer. Use for weaving or to include in a coiled basket. You may use it to tie twigs together, or even twist it into cordage.

Availability Grows naturally in some areas of Australia, but the better forms are now being seen in home gardens, as they are very striking when covered in the large blue form of hibiscus-like flowers. Most plant nurseries would have them.

Box thorn

box thorn hedge

Native hibiscus

Lavender (*Lavandula angustifolia, L. officinalis*)
FAMILY LABIATAE

Description This fragrant perennial herb grows in many gardens. The tall variety is better for our purposes than low growing forms because the stems are longer and sturdier.

To harvest Cut stems as long as you can when flower buds are beginning to open. The stems at this time are full of sap and less likely to break when doubled back. To dry, choose the longest stems with blossoms on or off, tie in bundles and hang to dry with heads down.

To use Tall lavender stems with flowers attached are used in basketry to make lavender sticks or wands. They can be used fresh, or collected and dried for use later on. To dampen dried stems for use, soak for several hours then wrap in a damp towel and leave overnight. If you want to use lavender in a coiled basket soak the starting stems very well, as they are most likely to break at the start of the coiling (see Lavender wands, page 69).

Availability Popular garden plant, often used to create hedges. Different varieties are grown in cottage and herb gardens and public places.

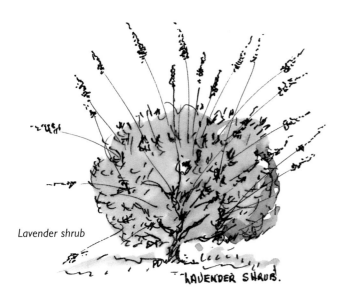

Lavender shrub

Wattles (*Acacias*)
FAMILY MIMOSACEAE

Watul is an old Anglo-Saxon word meaning a hurdle or shelter made from sticks woven together. The early European settlers in Australia discovered that they could use the pliable young stems of the native Acacias to make fences and houses by weaving or 'wattling' the stems to form house walls and then filling the gaps with wet clay or mud. From these early structures, now known as wattle-and-daub houses, the settlers gave the Acacia family the name Wattle.

With over 700 named wattle or Acacia species in Australia and at least 1100 around the world, the potential for these plants in basketry is still to be discovered. They are so diverse that you may find a use for your local wattle that has not yet been realised. It may be the leaves, as I mention in *Acacia dietrichiana*, or it may be the nice clean branches of *Acacia iteaphylla*, or perhaps the bark or the roots. Fibre from the inner bark can be removed and used for cordage. Refer to the *Encyclopaedia of Australian Plants* if you are interested in identifying your plants, as I can only describe one or two here. You will discover a variety in your garden or by the roadside that will respond with vigorous growth after you have given it a prune, and will probably wish to identify it.

Acacia dietrichiana

Description A common, hardy plant, 4–6 m tall; I first discovered this wattle's potential for basketry on a rainy day beside the river at Nyngan in north-western New South Wales. It was scrubby in habit and its long thin 'leaves' attracted my attention. (Wattles do not have true leaves but phyllodes, to be accurate.) In this species they are leathery with a prominent midvein. On picking some dry leaves from a dead branch, I found I could tie a knot in them.

To harvest Collect the longest leaves and dry them. You could collect from fallen branches if the leaves are in good condition.

To use Dampen by wrapping in a damp towel until pliable (this will not take very long).

The leaves may be stitched in the same way as coiled baskets (see page 56) or may be plaited or woven.

Availability Commonly found in central and northern Queensland, this wattle will be found growing on many station properties on rocky shallow soil. I am sure there are other dry country wattles that would be useful for craft work also. Why not grow some in your garden?

Gawler Range wattle (*Acacia iteaphylla*)

Description A dense, spreading medium shrub with attractive blue-green-grey foliage and showy bunches of small round pale yellow blossoms, the Gawler Range wattle is very popular as a garden plant. It has many forms. The weeping form tipped with pink on the new growth is the one I use.

To harvest Collect nice clean woody branches fresh from the shrub. These are most suitable for stakes and ribs. The long supple branches of some forms are very easy to cut and use when needed. I like to cut 1–2 days before use.

BOWL WITH HANDLE

Melon basket technique using twisted iris leaves and oak twig handle

Dramatic basket sculpture made from pussy willow rods, cordyline and dianella weavers

'Marge's Supplejack': ikebana basket made from clematis

Small melon basket with oak twig handle

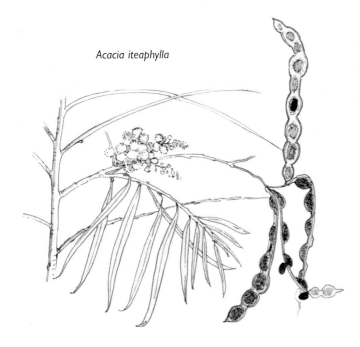

Acacia iteaphylla

To use Strip off the leaves and use within a week or two of collection. Pliable long lengths may be twisted into hoops or circles for a melon basket frame. It is hard yet flexible when fresh and can be twisted into shape and tied in place to dry. Clean lengths can be used for ribs.

Availability Native to South Australia, but a very popular small wattle for gardens or windbreaks.

TREES

Elm (*Ulmus* spp.)
Family Ulmaceae

Description Large ornamental trees, elms are vigorous and fast growing. They have been planted as street trees and in parks and large gardens all around the world. Since the 1930s elms in the the northern hemisphere have been decimated by a fungal disease.

To harvest and use The suckers or shoots can be cut at the lowest set of buds. By doing this you will encourage new growth to harvest the following year. As some may be quite tall clip off the longer lengths.

You may have access to a whole tree when one has to be removed, or a large limb may break off in a public park or old garden. If you see one being bulldozed, ask permission to collect some of the great assortment of roots at your disposal. You can also strip the bark from the fallen or cut branches and cut off any pliable shoots. I have included details below for harvesting each of the useable parts.

I find a Stanley knife a good tool for stripping bark, as you need to make cuts to start peeling the bark. When collecting bark at the tree the knife is very necessary. Cut around the branch at the bottom end, and then make a series of upward cuts. Pick up a corner of the bark and peel it up the branch as far as it will run. Collect as much as you want, wind it into coils and head for home. Prepare to spend some time separating the inner bark from the outer bark. You may slow the process down by keeping the bark under damp bags or let it dry and re-soak for use later.

Suckers or shoots These make great frame material and I find them very pliable. They can be bent into interesting shapes and tied in place until dry. Ideal for melon baskets, sculptural or circular wall pieces.

As you cut off a sucker, strip the bark away (it will pull away cleanly from the cut end), leaving a beautiful bleached branch or twig-like length. This adds to the appeal and decorative wall pieces are most attractive treated this way.

Branches Where branches have been lopped from large elm trees look for the pieces with long lengths that may suit the circles for a melon basket and its ribs. Take the bark off if you want or use the shoots *au naturel* with bark attached.

Outer bark The outer bark is also a useful material although more rugged in nature. It can add a rustic texture to weaving and can be used in most techniques. It can be coiled into bundles and allowed to dry, or, if used fresh, let some drying take place.

Inner bark Use a strong needle to assist you to slip the inner bark away. You will find it is like chamois leather, soft and very strong and pliable. You can plait it or twine it into string. Tie twigs and branches together.

Elm trees (English elm has a suckering habit)

The Native Americans used the inner bark to make baskets to hold water. It is strong and swells when wet.

I find it very useful material when I need something that is soft to work with but stiff or rigid when dry. Try and keep the material all the same size, then tie into bundles to store and dry. Soak the bark in water until it soft for re-use. Remove and wrap in a damp towel.

Roots Thin roots can be used as they are, or they are quite beautiful when stripped. The larger pieces may be bent and twisted but this must be done while the root is still fresh. The thick pieces of root can be shaped into handles or scylptural shapes and hung to dry. You may wish to wash this material before storing. Collect the roots and tie them into bundles, thin for weaving, thick for handles.

Root bark Strip the bark from the roots in even sized pieces. It comes away easily once started. Coil into bundles to use later when it has dried as there is a lot of shrinkage in this root bark. It becomes very slimy when soaked. Wipe with a damp towel if needed.

Inner root bark I think this bark is superior to the inner branch bark but of course it is not as readily available. Follow instructions for inner bark above.

Availability Parks, gardens and roadsides, as well as local recycling and refuse areas.

Kurrajong (*Brachychiton populneus*), Northern kurrajong (*B. diversifolius*)
FAMILY STERCULIACEAE

Description In the eastern states and the Northern Territory, kurrajongs grow as a tall shrub or small spreading tree with fissured grey bark. The leaves are shiny green above, dull beneath, and very variable in shape, from entire to five-lobed. The bell-shaped flowers are cream or pink. The pods are thick, leathery and dark brown.

The northern kurrajong has a slender trunk with striking flowers, deep red inside and furry yellow outside. It can be semi-deciduous depending on the rainfall.

Both roots and seeds were eaten by Aboriginal peoples.

To harvest
Pods The seed pods or cases are well known in shape and may be collected from the ground in gardens or from street plantings. Usually the seeds have been taken by a bird and several pods may be on one stem. The hard boat-shaped case has been likened to a red robin and use is often made of them as a novelty bird or pin cushion.
Bark The inner bark may be collected from a tree or log and was used by Aboriginal women to make a strong string. You must first remove the hard outer bark to get to the softer layers of inner bark and strip it off. This may be dried and stored and then dampened again for later use.

To use
Pods These can be stuffed with a small red 'pillow' to act as a pin cushion or make a robin, they may be painted and decorated and used in floral arrangements.
Bark The inner bark can be used when wet to make a strong tie or plied into a string for netted baskets or other uses.

Availability Garden plant or wild; kurrajongs may be found on stations as part of the bush or scrub. Popular as a shady street tree in warmer climates and well known in many areas of the world.

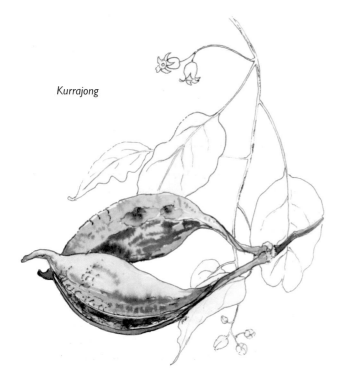

Kurrajong

Oak (*Quercus palustris, Q. alba*)
FAMILY FAGACEAE

Description Handsome trees with spreading branches, some oaks lose their leaves and colour up in autumn, others are evergreen. Their nuts are what most people know as acorns and this will help you identify them. The acorns may vary a little from one species to the next.

To harvest I have collected the lower branches from a pin oak in my garden, and found them extremely pliable and strong. The pin oak is less twiggy than some oaks and makes a cleaner handle. The bark holds on very well. Do this when it has dropped its leaves. Branches will remain pliable for several months if kept in a shaded place.

White oak is used in rural America, particularly in the Appalachian Mountains, for splint baskets. Saplings are split into quarters or eighths and the outer bark removed. A cleaning tool and mallet are used to remove the heartwood (this is often used for ribs and handles) and to split each piece into four at right angles to the growth rings.

Oak

Paperbark trunk

To use I select the branches I am going to use for a basket in the twig or melon technique, twist or tie them into the shape I want and hang them to dry for a short time before use. Trim off any branchlets you will not need. Short clean lengths can be used for ribs.

Availability Oak trees are found worldwide in parks, gardens and natural forest areas.

Paperbark (*Melaleuca cajoputi, M. stypheloides, M. dealbata, M. viridiflora*)
FAMILY MYRTACEAE

Description The Australian paperbark tree is known to most of us, once we see the lovely thick papery bark on the trunk. The bark can be an attraction in itself, as you can usually see the variation of colour, the softness and thickness, of this non-fibrous, sponge-like bark. Colours vary from almost white to grey with touches of pink, tan and even a greenish look to the areas covered with lichens.

To harvest Never damage the tree by taking a lot from the one area. You can gently push your fingers into the bark and pull a length away, or gently ease a longer length away from the trunk by pushing your fingers or a blunt knife along under the length required.

To use This material can be cut with scissors into strips and woven. It is well known for its use in Australia for bark pictures, where pieces of different colours are formed into a picture by gluing in the collage technique. Sheets of thick bark are used by Aboriginal peoples to make bush shelters, to sleep on or under, and to make food or water containers. In the past sheets of bark from the largest trees were traditionally used to wrap corpses for funeral ceremonies.

Ceremonial emblems are made in Northern Australia by rolling or folding the bark sheets and tightly bending the shape with hand-spun string. These may take the shapes of birds, plants or animals and are painted with ochres and decorated with string and feathers.

Dress barks were made on Groote Eylandt from two pieces of bark approximately 60 cm x 80 cm (24" x 30") stitched down the short side with *Flagellaria indica* (lawyer vine). The women carried them on their heads, and would cover themselves if a man other than their husband approached.

The roots, which are sometimes exposed after flooding, can be used in coiled and woven work.

Availability Gardens, parks and some forested areas. The bark is sold in rolls to line hanging baskets in some supermark ets and garden suppliers.

She-oak (*Allocasuarina* spp.)
FAMILY CASUARINACEAE

Description There are over thirty species of Allocasuarina; many of them have slender branchlets (or leaves as most people would view them) that can be up to 50 cm (20") long. Similar in appearance to a drooping

'Leaves' of she-oak

pine, they can be shrubs or trees. I have a form of A. cunninghamiana in my garden with branchlets up to 50 cm (20") long but I also have several others of that species which do not grow long branchlets and are not as useful. The fruits are woody cones. This material is extremely useful for stitched coiled work or woven basketry.

To harvest Look for a tree with branchlets 20 cm (8") and longer. You can collect from the ground or collect from the tree. Pull the branchlets from the plant with an upward tug. Tie them into small bundles and allow to dry for most uses. Their shrinkage is not great, so in drier areas it is possible to coil them while fresh.

To use Dampen for use by wrapping in a damp towel. This does not take long. I have found this material to be very pliable at most times with very little wetting. I use the branchlets in mixed media work with a length of bark or rush, including several pieces of she-oak as I twine. It gives colour and texture variation.

This is excellent material for coiled work, used as a core and then stitched. Stems with branchlets attached may be tied into circles or other shapes and lightly stitched or wrapped to make wreaths.

Availability Used as decorative plantings in parks and gardens. Collect from the ground in public places. A species native to Australia and not difficult to find in South-East Asia and many other areas.

Willows—Golden willow (*Salix alba vitellina*), Weeping golden willow (*S. chrysocams*), Weeping willow (*S. babylonica*), Pussy willow (*S. discolor*), Chilean willow (*S. chilensis*), Basket willow (*S. amybdaline*), Narrow-leafed willows (*S. alba, S. fragilis, S. triandra, S. viminalis*)
FAMILY SALICACEAE

Description These rapidly growing trees and shrubs are many in type; but probably the best known is the green weeping willow. This has naturalised in much of Australia in damp places, as have many of the shrubby forms, along swamps and streams. I like the golden willow. It is easily recognised when it loses its leaves as the stems are a golden colour. This comes in a weeping and a more upright form. It is difficult to identify many of the willows—they just look like a willow to most people—but in Australia they have cross-bred and we now have as many as 27 different sorts. In fact, there is a willow invasion in some areas and people are glad to have them cut down.

FRESH WILLOW
To harvest I like to collect willow in the autumn, when the sap is going down, before the tree becomes dormant in winter, but you may find it different in your area. Some people harvest it in spring when the sap is on the rise, and at this stage it is easy to peel the bark off, if you wish to have this cleaner look. The bark can also be saved for use.

You will enjoy using this material when it is freshly cut as it can be used for stakes or ribs, framework and also as weaving material. Remember though that natural materials are not uniform, so that a branch of willow may not yield perfect weaving lengths. Some may break, or they may not be flexible near the thicker end. It is the cleaner younger growth that is useable. Give your local willows a prune to encourage nice new growth for later use.

To use The weeping golden willow and some forms of the green weeping willow provide very pliable weaving material, with the golden form drying to a very nice orange brown bark. Pussy willow is also very good to use.

Willow twigs can be split so they may be used for finer weaving. You will need to practice this. Start the split with a cut and then pull down carefully.

The basket willow is more upright and has long smooth lengths about finger thickness that may be used for framework. Look at the willows in your area and try bending the finer lengths around your finger at various points along the stem. You will soon find out if it is suitable for weaving or framework. My local willows are my main source of supply for melon baskets, providing ribs, framework and fine golden willow for weaving. In many countries willow baskets (the stake and strand method) were made by farmers to take their produce to market.

Willow has been farmed and sold commercially in England for many years. I know of a golden willow on a

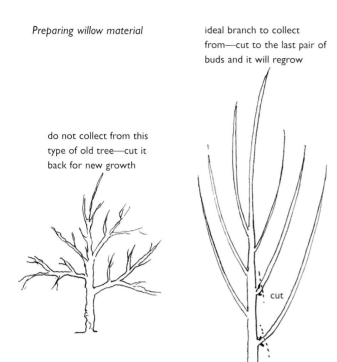

Preparing willow material

do not collect from this type of old tree—cut it back for new growth

ideal branch to collect from—cut to the last pair of buds and it will regrow

cut

cut

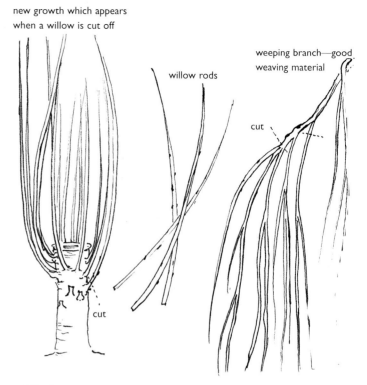

new growth which appears when a willow is cut off

willow rods

weeping branch—good weaving material

cut

cut

farm owned by an Italian-Australian family which was planted planted three generations ago by the first member of the family, who carried the cutting from his village in Italy to Australia because he could not imagine how otherwise he would get his produce to market.

PROCESSED WILLOW

To harvest Willow for processing is gathered in winter when the sap is down. It is processed into three different 'colours'. Brown willow is left to dry with the bark on. For white willow the bark is peeled off and the rods left to dry. Buff coloured willow is boiled for several hours in large vats to allow the tannin from the bark to stain the wood. The bark is then peeled off and the rods left to dry ('rod' is the term used for the lengths of willow in basketry—it may also be applied to material other than willow that has not been split). The tannin acts as a preservative. Processed willow is then tied into 'bolts' and sold in different lengths.

To use Soak the willow rods for 2–3 hours and wrap in a thick wet cloth or towel for another two hours. They should then be ready to use. Willow rods are thick at one end and thin at the other, so willow is quite different from cane to use. Cane remains flexible and curves, where willow will kink. Because the rods are uneven in thickness, you will have to be aware and to keep your weaving even. You will need to keep butts to butts and tips to tips. If using several weavers together choose rods of an uneven length so that they both do not run out together.

Availability Parks, gardens and naturalised in wet areas.

VINES AND CREEPERS

Clematis, Traveller's joy, Old man's beard, Mountain clematis, Goat's beard (*Clematis aristata*), Forest clematis (*C. glycinoides*), Small-leafed clematis (*C. microphylla*)
FAMILY RANUNCULACEAE

Description The common names for the mountain clematis (*C. aristata*) include supplejack, used by farmers in southern Victoria. The vine is so pliable it can be used to tie up a gate. In areas of high rainfall this vine is one of the first colonisers of a regenerated forest and soon scrambles up small shrubs and trees, creating areas of jungle-like vines as it grows towards the light. When in flower we see the bunches of creamy white star-like flowers, hanging from the branch of a tree or shrub, and then the seeds follow with long silky beards. When grown in the home garden it can be quite vigorous if its feet are planted in the shade, and it will stand cutting back every few years to regenerate again.
C. glycinoides or forest clematis, found along the east coast of Victoria, New South Wales and Queensland in moist sheltered areas, is of similar vigour, a wonderful long vine.
C. microphylla loves dry places and grows from the coast inland in temperate Australia

To harvest When the vine is mature (2–3 years growth or more) it has a lovely dark gnarled look to it and is so flexible you can use the thicker parts to twist a handle for a basket and the thinner lengths to weave with. It is a joy to use. When collecting it can be twisted into coils and

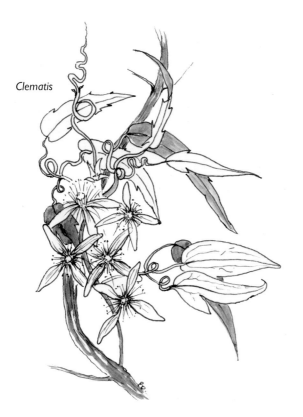

Clematis

To harvest Strip off the leaves and twist the vine into loose coils. Let it shrink for about a week before use. Keep it in a shady spot.

To use For best results use coral pea before it completely dries out, but it can be soaked for an hour and wrapped in a damp towel overnight.

The older parts of these vines can be wonderful for framework and decorative handles. If you have access to an old vine, you will find it extremely pliable and great to work with. I rate it among the best there is for sculptural work. When the vine is about finger thickness, it becomes quite dark in colour and can have beautiful twists in it that can be shown to advantage in handles or wall pieces. *K. nigricans* will grow very thick stems around its base; these can be cut from an old plant as sculptural pieces.

Availability Common in garden plantings. After my first plant died (and became a basket), I found seedlings popping up for years after, so I always have several scrambling around my garden. Just look and you will see this plant or other members of its family growing on fences and used to cover banks and trees. An Australian native.

dried. As a garden plant it can be cut back quite severely and will then start up again, allowing you a constant supply.

To use Use fresh or, if dried, soak to soften. This may take quite some time and it may not be as easy to work as when fresh. Your could twist any older vine into handle shapes and allow to dry, to use later for a melon basket combined with fresh material. Vine may also be split for weaving if needed.

Availability *C. aristata* is widespread in dry scrub to wet sclerophyll forest. It is a very popular garden plant and widely cultivated. *C. glycinoides* is not as widely grown as *C. aristata*. *C. microphylla* is the most widespread species in dry scrub and heathland. It is popular in cultivation as a garden plant.

Coral Pea, Black or Dusky (*Kennedia nigricans, K. rubicunda, K. macrophylla*)
FAMILY FABACEAE

Description This family of climbing plants has become very popular in our gardens, to cover large fences and provide windbreaks. They generally have a large leaf that looks a bit clover-like; the flowers are black or red and orange pea flowers which can be very showy. These plants can become so vigorous they wear out their welcome. They should be pruned after flowering and that is the time to ask your neighbours for the prunings. The vines make superb weaving material, being very pliable and strong.

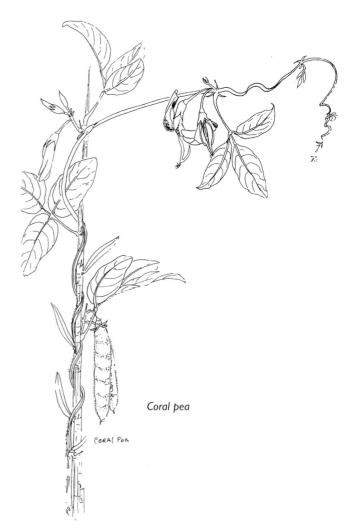

Coral pea

CORAl PeA

Dodder laurel, Tangled dodder (*Cassytha glabella*),
Downy dodder laurel (*C. pubescens*), Coarse
dodder laurel (*C. melantha*), Slender dodder
(*C. capillaris*)
FAMILY LAURACEAE

Description I have seen fine and coarse forms of this
plant growing in most states of Australia. It also occurs in
New Guinea, Indonesia, Sri Lanka, North and South
America and southern Africa. It can create a 'spooky'
impression when you see it along roadsides, as it drapes
over small trees and shrubs, hanging, tangled and heavy,
and at times bending the tree over, until the dodder
actually slips off or breaks the tree. I have seen it so thick
in some areas that the host shrubs have been killed and
the dodder itself has died.

A leafless parasitic plant, dodder laurel has tangled
stems with clusters of tiny greenish white flowers. It can be
quite attractive as its colour varies from greenish yellow to
orange. As it dries it becomes more brown-orange. It has
small round white fruits that are ripe when clear, loved by
Australian Aboriginal children and also used in Asia.

To harvest I collect dodder by pulling it off the tree in
great thick tangled masses, coiling it roughly and then
cutting it off with clippers. Coil it into bundles and store
in a cardboard box.

To use Dodder can be pulled apart and used as a core in
a coiled and stitched basket. Let it dry a few weeks before
using it for coiling, as it does shrink as it dries.

I prefer to use dodder for weaving in a melon basket
technique. Leave it in thick rope-like lengths, twisting it
to weave in and out and over the stakes. It gives a lovely
bird's-nest effect and is really quite strong. It can be used
fresh in this type of basket.

Dodder is a very useful material for large sculptural
works because of the quantities that can be found and
bound into wreaths for floral art work.

If dry soak about half and hour before use.

Availability Frequently found in small bush gardens, or
in large areas of bush. People may be glad to have you
collect it in some areas as it can become a pest.

Fuchsia, Prostrate (*Fuchsia procumbens*)
FAMILY ONAGRACEAE

Description This attractive prostrate scrambler will grow
in shady conditions. Its long fine wiry stems are covered
with bright green heart-shaped leaves. Its tiny bell-shaped
flowers are gold with a green turnback on the petals; the
striking stamens are orange with blue anthers. It has been
sold as a hanging basket plant, and seems to lose a lot of
leaf in winter.

To harvest You will be able to collect long runners from
this plant as they find their way amongst the leaf litter
and low plants. I collect it from my garden and store in a
shady spot, but it can be used fresh.

To use You can weave or twine with this dainty strong
material. It adds a pleasant rustic look to projects, and I
like to use several strands together. It can dry tan to dark
brown in colour.

Availability This plant is sold in hanging baskets, or as a
prostrate groundcover or rockery plant. A useful garden
plant and groundcover.

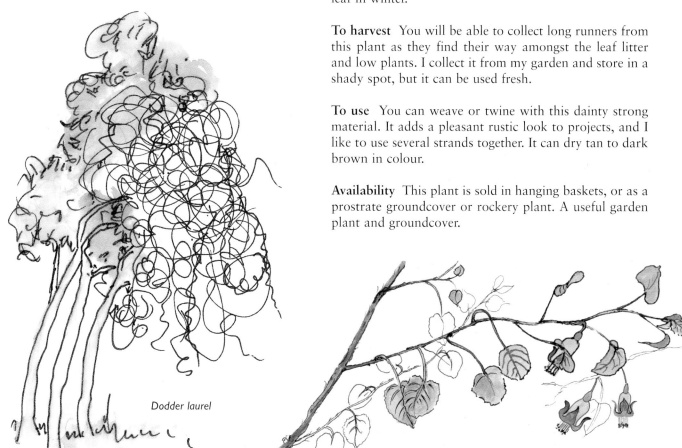

Dodder laurel

Fuchsia procumbens

Ivy (*Hedera helix*)
FAMILY ARALIACEAE

Description Evergreen woody-stemmed trailing perennials and self-clinging climbers with roughly triangular, usually lobed leaves.

To harvest Harvest this vine when you are nearly ready to use it. Find the long runners (growing in shade and through mulch or grass) or cut runners where they might hang over a fence. Do not collect where it has roots and attached itself to a fence or wall, as these parts are usually brittle. The exception would be where an old ivy has grown beautiful sculptural root clumps.

To use The runners can be very pliable and strong, great to use in weaving or to tie twigs with; the root clumps can make a very decorative feature when added to a piece of work, e.g. the top or side of a basket or wall hanging.

You can boil the runners to remove the bark. Do this by coiling small bundles roughly, and placing them in boiling water for 10–30 minutes. Test before removing to see if you can slip the bark off the stem. A cotton gardening glove on your hand will make this much easier. Dry the vine, and you will have a very nice bleached cane-like weaving material. You can dye this material at this stage.

Availability Common garden plant, often escaped to roadsides, banks and streams.

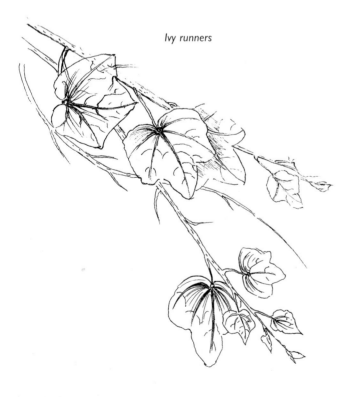

Ivy runners

Jasmine (*Jasminum officinale*)
FAMILY OLEACEAE

Description Semi-evergreen, twining climber, with clusters of fragrant white flowers in summer to autumn. Can grow to 12 m (40"). Several related varieties are grown, but this form is the best for weaving.

To harvest I prefer to collect the long runners that lead off along the ground in shady places. These have very few leaves and can be clipped off in large amounts. Plants that have grown in a very dry position tend to grow in a twiggy tangled way, so you will not find a lot of useful vine.

To use Jasmine gives best results if used fresh when picked or left a few days to allow some shrinkage. It

Jasmine

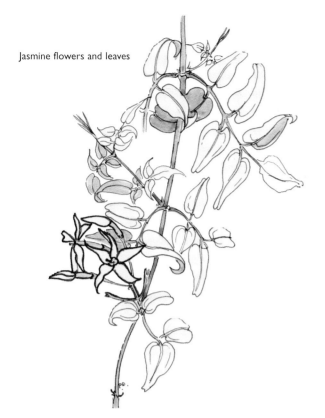

Jasmine flowers and leaves

Lawyer vine

does stay pliable for some time, if kept in a dry shady spot.

I use this vine for basket making where I need a neat regular finish. It is excellent for starting a melon basket and for wherever a good strong wrapped finish is needed.

If twisted into wreaths jasmine can be dried and stored for a base for a later project, e.g. Christmas wreaths.

Availability A well known plant, common in gardens. Owners are only too glad to have you ask for some, as it can get out of control in the right conditions.

Lawyer vine, Climbing bamboo, Supplejack (*Fragellaria indica*)
FAMILY FRAGELLARIACEAE

Description This climber has long flexible shoots with tendrils on the leaf ends to assist climbing. It is robust and will reach 15 m (50') long. It grows in monsoon vine forest, around wet areas, mangroves and open forests and woodlands. It has creamy white bunches of flowers at the ends of its branches, followed by fleshy round fruits that change from dark green to pink when ripe. I saw this plant growing as a huge clump beside a waterhole. It had scrambled partly up a tree and mostly around itself. The vine looks like a thin rattan but much more flexible.

To harvest Cut canes and use soon after collection or twist into bracelets or wreaths that can be stored to dry for later use.

To use The Australian Aborigines made good use of this plant. The stems were split into four, softened by soaking in water and used to sew bark coolamons. Thicker stems were split and used to sew bark canoes. This could be used to build a frame and the finer lengths for weaving.

Availability You may have access to this plant if it is being cleared from public places or on private property.

Lignum (*Muehlenbeckia florulentia*), Tangled lignum (*M. cunninghamii*), Twiggy lignum (*M. diclina*)
FAMILY POLYGONACEAE

Description Slender sprawling shrubs with yellow or whitish green flowers, these unusual looking plants grow in the lignum swamps (those areas where river overflows create swampy areas for a while, before drying up again), often growing in association with cane grass. After rain the lignum will grow rapidly, suckering to expand the area of the parent clump. It has no obvious leaves, but does have flowers at the tops of the new shoots, rather insignificant but nonetheless a flowering spray. The smooth cane-like growths can be straight and a mid-green colour at first, changing to a grey-green as they mature. They grow in a tangled untidy sort of way, but never twine or climb, so can be easily harvested. The plant can be up to 3 m (10") tall.

To harvest This material can be collected after a vigorous growing period, and long lengths twisted into small circles and coiled into wreaths for later use. The older parts of the plant are more suited to cutting and drying as

Lignum

Native raspberry

straight pieces. If used this way it is important to allow shrinkage to take place by drying.

To use Lignum is probably only useful for framework and ribs. It dries similar to bamboo, so when coiled and dried it should not be unwound. It could provide framework for small melon baskets, Christmas wreaths and so on; dried in straight lengths, it could be used to make a structure (e.g. sculptural) by tying the crosspieces.

Availability In swamps and floodplains in inland Australia.

Native raspberry (*Rubus parvifolius*)
FAMILY ROSACEAE

Description A small slender spreading plant which scrambles around like a miniature blackberry. It also has tiny prickles on stems and leaves. The small dark pink berries are edible.

To harvest Wear strong gardening gloves when collecting this vine and wipe off the prickles.

To use Can be used for small wreaths or woven baskets. It is very pliable especially when runners have been covered by dense grass. Allow shrinkage time. I would keep a watch on the material, testing it by bending and as soon as it starts to dry, use it for weaving and twining. You may be able to make small berry baskets in the melon basket technique with some of the older vine, if you have an abundance.

Availability Still quite common in south-eastern Australia on the sloping edges of roadsides; clumps can be found in patches of bush, around old buildings and in forested areas. Also found in China and Japan.

Wait-a-while, Lawyer vine, Rattan canes
(*Calamus australis, C. caryotoides, C. moti, C. muelleri, C. radicans*)
(see also Lawyer vine or Flagellaria)
FAMILY ARECACEAE

Description One of the climbing palms whose stems have millions of tiny sharp hooks, *C. australis* is a vigorous climbing palm with pale green fronds 2–3 m (6'–10') long. As the wind blows the tendrils around, they come in contact with one or other of the surrounding rainforest plants, to which they hold on firmly, and grow upwards towards the light. As the stems grow older the thorns disappear, and they become lawyer vines or rattan canes which are used for basketry, furniture, etc. The common name of wait-a-while is appropriate, as you must do just that—wait a while—until you disengage yourself from all those hooks. This palm is sometimes grown as an indoor pot plant in temperate Australia. It is a rapid grower in places like Indonesia, where it is now protected as its export value is realised. The different varieties grow canes from pencil thickness to thicker than a broom handle.

To use Use green as it is more pliable. It can be split to use if too thick, or soaked in hot water to bend for handles. Short lengths are usually available from craft outlets for use as handles for cane baskets. The better quality canes make a superior basket, both in strength and colour; the smoothness of the canes (when stripped of the outer prickly skin) can make for comfortable chairs, stools and small tables. This material is mostly worked by men as they have the extra strength in their hands to bend and cut the canes continuously. Leave the basket or chair to dry.

Wait-a-while

Availability These plants grow in northern area of Australia, South-East Asia and the tropics. Some basket makers in Northern Australia use this material and collect it themselves, but it is available as an import from Asia and it is much easier to purchase it from cane wholesalers than to collect it. I went collecting in North Queensland years ago, when my daughter was on a property near Port Douglas, but I lost my desire rather rapidly when I was showered with green ants. It is protected in some areas of rainforest now and a permit will be needed to collect from other areas. There are quite healthy stands of it to be seen in National Parks in the wet tropics, particularly in Queensland.

Wisteria (*Wisteria* spp.)
FAMILY FABACEAE

Description A deciduous, vigorous, climbing vine, very showy when in flower and well known for its long drooping bunches of mauve-blue flowers. Some forms have white flowers.

To harvest
Runners You will need access to an older vine, as this will have long rope-like runners the thickness of your finger. Where these runners go off into the shade, they have no leaves or flowers. These lengths make superb basketry material and are ideal to collect and use fresh for weaving. Cut them with sharp secateurs and coil them into circles for transporting. Owners are usually glad for you to offer to take wisteria away, as it is a big job to do when pruning in the autumn. Collect the gnarled and twisted lengths to make wonderful frames and twist the decorative pieces into circles for melon basket handles.
Bark The bark may also be used, as it strips off very well and can be used for finer weaving or tying and plaiting. If you are patient, you can also separate the inner bark, which is very fine and pliable.

To use Most times this vine will be clean, but can have sharp, hard little nodes in some places that need clipping off as soon as possible after pruning. Keep in a shady cool spot to keep the moisture in. The vine will stay pliable for quite some time, giving you time to work through a large quantity of it.

Young canes, up to one year old, can be used but are mostly too brittle to weave, as in a melon basket. They can be twisted into wreaths easily.

Finger thickness vine is wonderful material for large works if you can get the quantity. Use after it has been cut for a week or so. The longer you can leave it the better.

Old plants have beautiful gnarled parts that can be selectively cut for handles or special sculptured work. I have used this to make a huge basket, 1 m x 70 cm (40" x 28") in size. The heaviness of the green material will cause the basket to slump as it dries, so be aware.

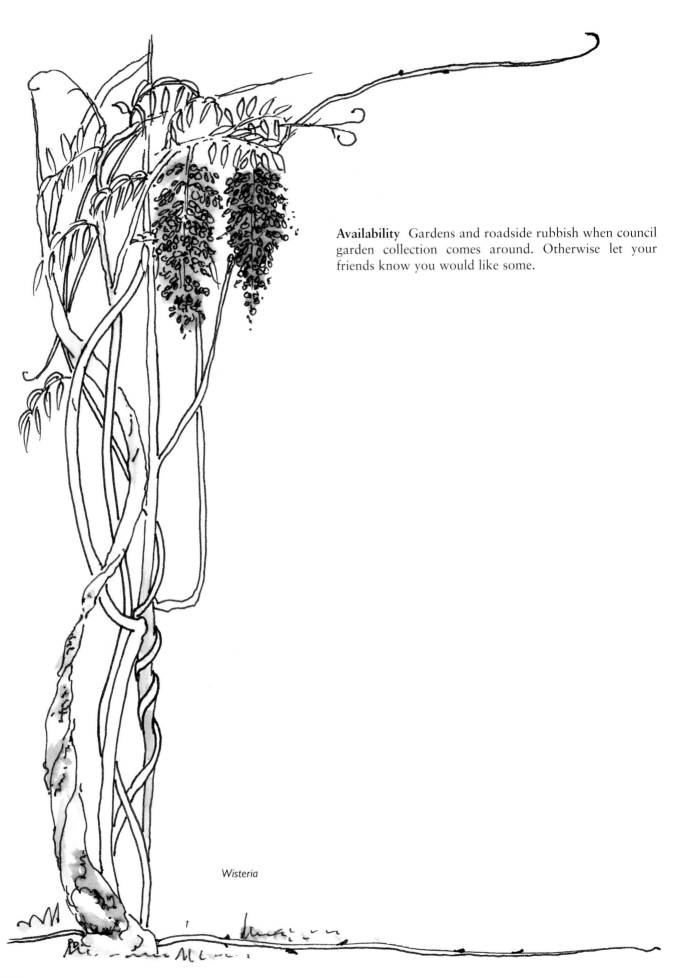

Availability Gardens and roadside rubbish when council garden collection comes around. Otherwise let your friends know you would like some.

Wisteria

3 techniques to get you started

The techniques I have included in this book are mostly borrowed from basketry. Traditionally basket makers and weavers used the materials that were available in their own environment, and they developed techniques to suit their local materials.

I have found the melon basket technique suits our modern day lifestyle beautifully, for it allows you to build a frame and cover it in; you can become very skilled at adapting it, making it functional or decorative at will. You will need to keep in mind though, if you want a thing to hold together without nails or glue, that time spent learning a few good techniques is time well spent.

But as I have found, it's a lot more fun to break the rules now and then.

UNDER AND OVER WEAVING—WEAVE A TABLE MAT

Materials

- Select 18–20 bulrushes (dried and dampened), 50 cm (20") long, cut from top end of bulrush
- Use house brick covered with fabric to hold rushes in place
- Scissors

Following the diagrams:

Place half the rushes on the table, side by side. Place the brick on top of them (A) to hold them in place

Fold each alternate rush back over brick and begin weaving by placing another rush across the flat rushes (B). Take the folded rushes back and bring the remaining rushes forward. Lay a new rush across the flat ones, then return bent rushes to the flat position (C). Continue in this way, leaving about 8 cm (3") of rush to turn in (D).

Move brick onto woven area and turn weaving so you can repeat to the other end.

Lay the finished mat under some heavy books for a day.

START A SCULPTURAL PIECE

Set up a frame to weave over, using vine or twigs. Following the diagram:

The weaver can be vines, dried leaves, bark or willow. Try to keep an even tension on your weaving so that you do not close the frame up by pulling too tightly.

Different effects can be obtained by choosing thick or thin material to weave with. Short, textured lengths of bark can be laid or woven in alongside the weaver.

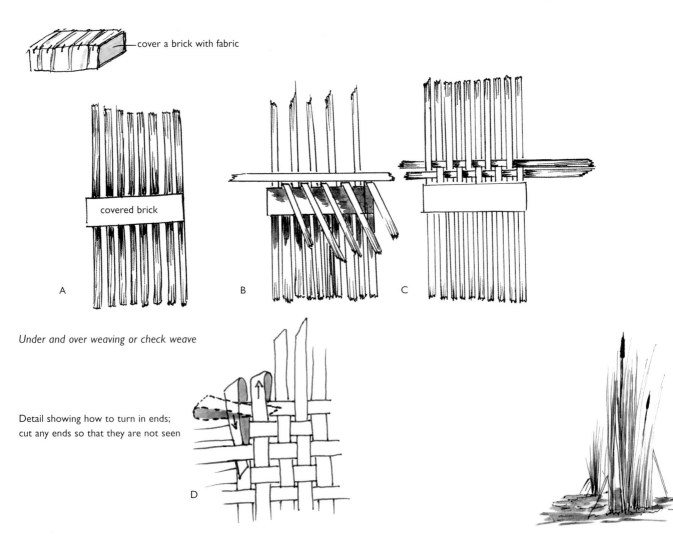

cover a brick with fabric

covered brick

A   B   C

Under and over weaving or check weave

Detail showing how to turn in ends; cut any ends so that they are not seen

D

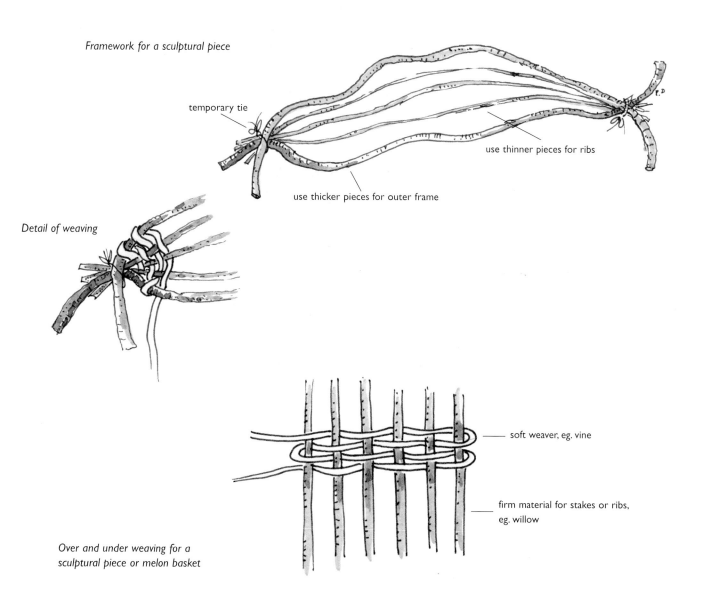

Framework for a sculptural piece

temporary tie

use thinner pieces for ribs

use thicker pieces for outer frame

Detail of weaving

soft weaver, eg. vine

firm material for stakes or ribs, eg. willow

Over and under weaving for a sculptural piece or melon basket

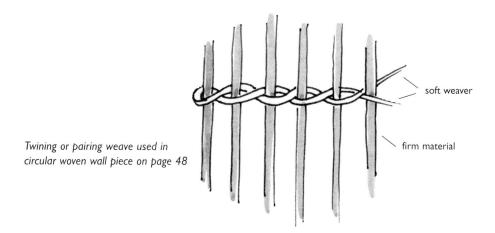

soft weaver

firm material

Twining or pairing weave used in circular woven wall piece on page 48

CIRCULAR WOVEN WALL PIECE

Use willow or similar material for stakes. Weavers can be jasmine or ivy vines. You may like to add in such things as bark or seaweed alongside the weaver to add colour or texture.

Note on seaweed: When you collect seaweed take it straight home and wash in warm soapy water, rinse, and hang to dry on a tree or fence. It can then be stored away. Dampen in water to soften again to weave with.

Following the diagrams:
To start, take six or eight stakes not more than 50 cm (20") long. Weave two rows following the diagram and then weave around each stake with the same technique.

Finish off the two weavers by slipping or pulling them down beside the nearest stake. Make sure they are secure and at least four rows down.

New Zealand flax leaf, very finely split with a darning needle, can be attached to the centre of the disc or hung from the ends of the stakes

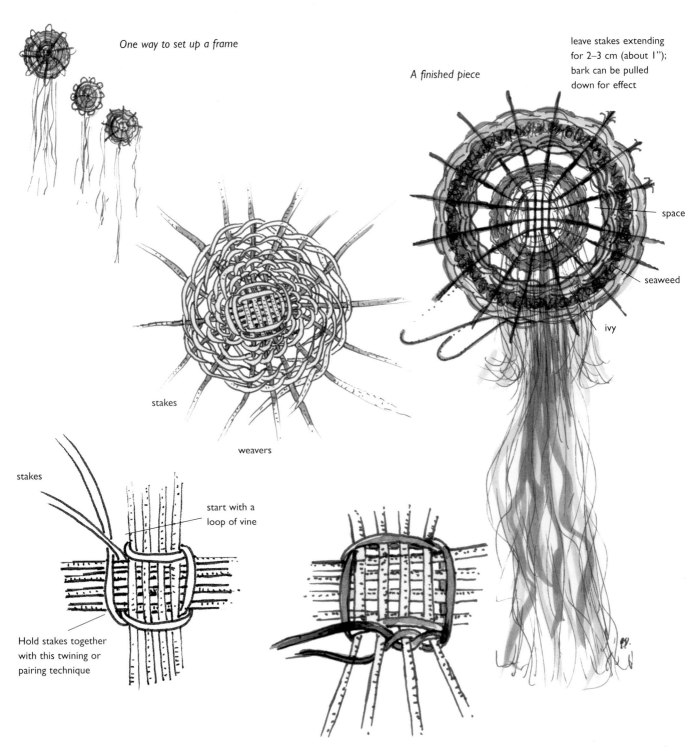

One way to set up a frame

A finished piece

leave stakes extending for 2–3 cm (about 1"); bark can be pulled down for effect

space

seaweed

ivy

stakes

weavers

stakes

start with a loop of vine

Hold stakes together with this twining or pairing technique

Opening the stakes out to become circular

This metre-long basket is made from a very old wisteria vine, with some particularly lovely pieces used in the handle

Made from oak twigs and woven with bulrush, kennedia, prostrate fuchsia, day lily and the bright tan of watsonia leaves. Note the variety of natural colours. The greens will eventually fade to grey

COILED PLATTER

Coiled platter of bulrush and cordyline butts stitched with jute string

Tassels as curtain ties. The upper two are made from bulrush, the one at the bottom from day lily leaves. Note the decorative plaited cording

BRAIDING OR PLAITING WITH THREE STRANDS

The leaves most suitable for this plait are iris, day lily, red-hot poker, gladiolus, rushes. See notes on pages 15, 13, 22 and 16 for preparation, and the section Plaited and sewn autumn mat, pages 72-73. Top and tail the leaves, so you don't have all the thin ends together, and the plait should end up an even thickness (A). Give the leaves a twist as you plait, if you like (B). Join in a new rush or leaf by laying in the new one over the old, trimming off any ends. Alternate the tip and butt ends.

With the completed plait you can cover a wooden stool, make a cat basket, a log basket for the fireplace . .

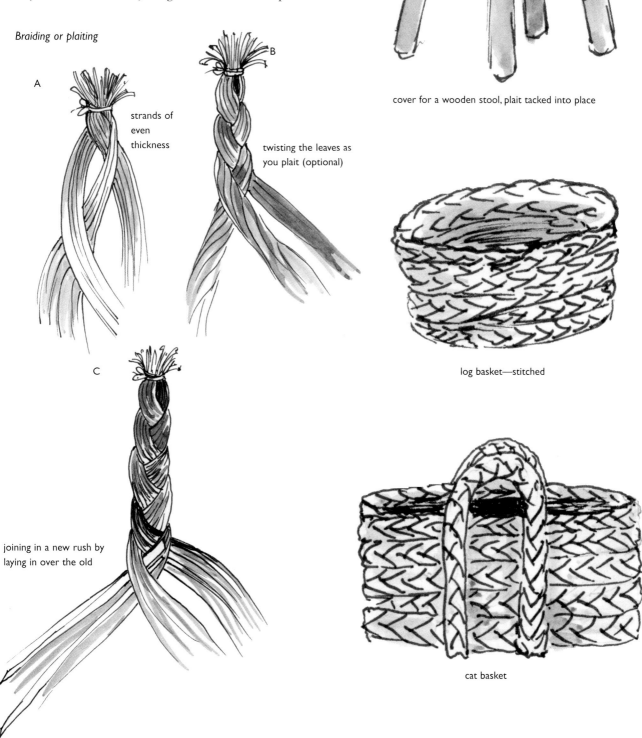

Braiding or plaiting

A

strands of
even
thickness

B

twisting the leaves as
you plait (optional)

C

joining in a new rush by
laying in over the old

cover for a wooden stool, plait tacked into place

log basket—stitched

cat basket

BASIC MELON BASKET CONSTRUCTION

This technique is ideal for your first 'constructed frame' basket.

Materials

Frame Needs to be two strong circles approximately 25 cm (10") in diameter, or 6–8 rods. You can use a nice twisted vine for a handle. Make one circle plain, the other decorative.

Rods Any single length that has not been split, e.g. as found in willow or elm tree suckers. Privet or fruit tree trimmings (plums are great) are also useful.

Stakes or ribs Eight long rods under 7.5 mm thick and not twiggy.

Weaving The materials used for weaving over the frame need to be very pliable and as long as possible. You can never have too much! Vines and creepers can be found everywhere if you go looking, e.g. ivy, jasmine, wisteria, kennedia, clematis, New Zealand flax. Dried leaves if you have started collecting, e.g. day lily, cumbungi, iris, red-hot poker. Dampen to use. See Other useful materials, page 75.

Method

Step 1 Make two circles of similar size. Choose nice twisted pieces for the handle; a circle about 25 cm (10") in diameter would be a good size for your first basket.

Step 2 You can tie circles together where marked. This is only a temporary measure. Tie a small bow on the 'handle'. (People do forget the handle.)

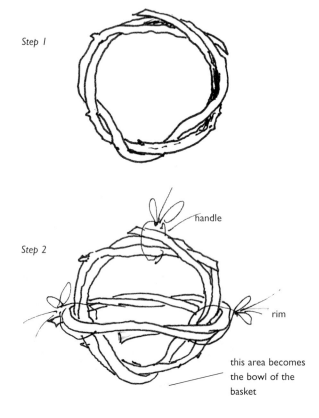

Basic melon basket construction

Step I

Step 2

handle

rim

this area becomes the bowl of the basket

Step 3 Use a small length of New Zealand flax (or string) for these ties, which are only temporary. Small section of weaving at both ends. Select a length of fine pliable material for weaver, e.g. vine, or a long dried leaf, e.g. day lily, dampened. Start as per diagram 3. Have woven 'rows' side by side until you have approximately 3–4 cm (1¼"–1½") each side of frame—just enough. You will only need enough weaving to hold ribs. Use clothes peg to hold vine in place at each end, to stop work unravelling.

This area will form a figure 8 as the vine crosses to go to the opposite side. These spaces—two each side—are where the ribs will sit in. You may place two ribs in each space, thus having four ribs on each side of basket bowl.

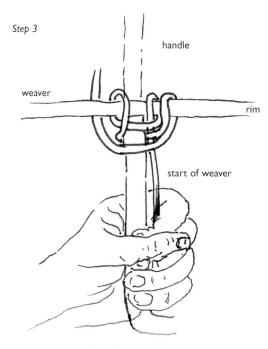

Step 3

handle

weaver

rim

start of weaver

Step 4 Setting in the ribs Cut 6–8 ribs, measuring from weaving to weaving and under basket frame to get approximate length. Cut a wedge on ends. Slip them into the weaving as per the diagram. Now adjust each rib to shape your basket. I make the two under the basket longer to provide a base for it to sit on, and shorten the others as needed.

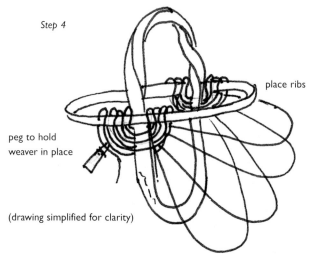

Step 4

place ribs

peg to hold weaver in place

(drawing simplified for clarity)

Step 5 *Weaving* Unclip weaver. Continue weaver on and weave it under and over each rib including frame. Choose some fine very pliable long lengths, to set the ribs in place; complete two rows on each end. This is important to hold the piece together. Then weave about 4 cm (1¹/₂") each time before turning to opposite end.

Extra ribs may be added if you have a large gap.

To join in a weaver Find a spot near the centre of the basket and lay a new one beside the end of the old. If they travel along over two ribs it will make a strong join.

Weaving material Choose from the list; you can create your own multi-coloured basket if you choose an assortment of materials, thinking about colour and texture and weaving with several weavers together as you find the ribs get further apart.

Now continue weaving from end to end—you must finish in the centre of the basket. You may distort the basket shape if you do not finish in the centre, especially when working with fresh material. Make sure you pack your weaving firmly at the finish, so that you do not have a hole in the basket. Leave the basket to dry in a dry warm spot; this takes about six weeks. If your basket doesn't 'sit' well, place some newspaper in the bottom and fill with oranges or potatoes, anything with weight, and the basket will settle down as it dries.

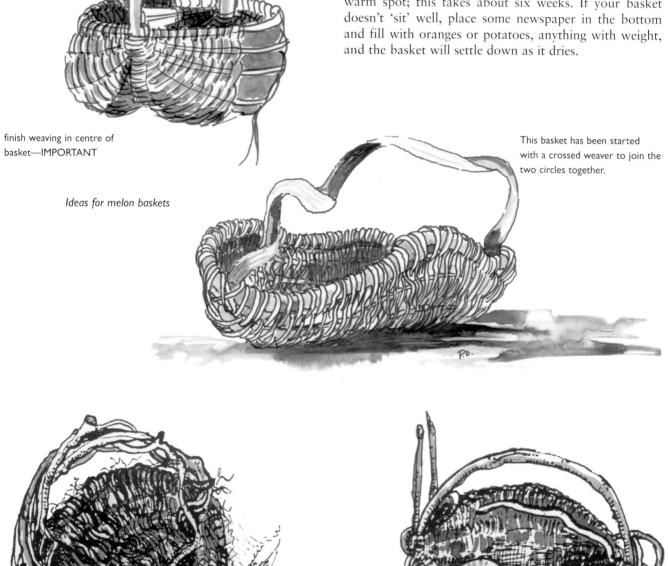

Step 5

finish weaving in centre of basket—IMPORTANT

Ideas for melon baskets

This basket has been started with a crossed weaver to join the two circles together.

COILING A BASKET WITH EASY RANDOM STITCHING

This basket is made by stitching a bundle of leaves or grasses, called the core, into a coil. The core is coiled round and round and sewn lightly with an oversew stitch to the coil beneath. When you have made your basket this way, you may like to try several of the various other decorative stitches used in coiled work for your next piece.

Materials

Needle—a tapestry, chenille or darning needle with a large eye is best
Thread—raffia or linen
Scissors
Leaves (illustration A)

Following the diagrams:

To prepare Make sure the leaves you select for your basket are well dried. Dampen the material before you start (illustration B). Try not to dampen more than you need, as it may become mildewed. I suggest day lily, corn husks, iris or similar.

Thread your needle with your choice of thread (if it is raffia, split the length of raffia into 3 or 4 finer lengths). I like to wipe the sewing thread through a damp cloth or dip it in water, to help resist twists.

To start The centre of the coil is started with just two or three leaves and gradually added to as you move into the second row. Start with three day lily leaves, iris leaves or corn cob husks. Use these softer materials for your first attempt, and then move onto pine needles, bark, or flax after your first coiled basket. I personally find the long soft leaves really relaxing to use.

Hold leaves together at tip end, twist them together a little and then trim off soft tips on an angle.

Taking the needle and thread, and holding leaves about 1 cm (3/8") back from the tip ends (illustration C), catch the end of the thread under your thumb along the leaves. You can make a loop and knot around the leaves at this point, then proceed to wrap the thread around the leaves, moving backwards along the bunch of leaves about 4–5 cm (1½"–2"). This start can just as easily be

Coil a basket with easy random stitching

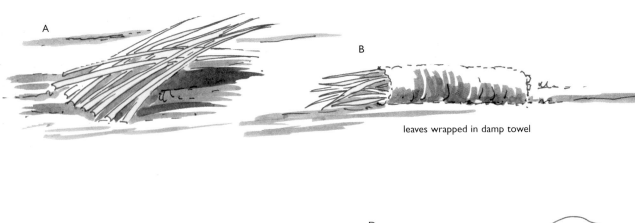

A

B

leaves wrapped in damp towel

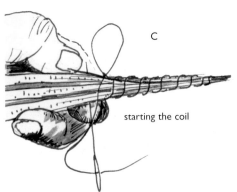

C

starting the coil

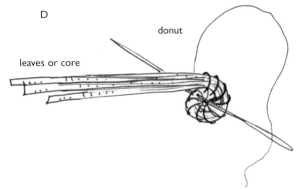

D

donut

leaves or core

made by starting 4–5 cm (1½"–2") back from the tip ends and wrapping thread towards the tip, then making the 'donut'. You will find the method you prefer with experience.

Now loop the core around the starting point and make a 'donut' (illustration D). Wrap around your little circle and make a secure join. Try to avoid leaving a large hole in the centre. You are now ready to add to your core. Open up the leaves as shown in illustration E and lay in the leaf or leaves, increasing the thickness of the core fairly quickly now, every 2–3 stitches, until you have the thickness you require. I think finger thickness is a good sized core to start with. You will need to have your supply of plant material on hand, as you will be picking up constantly to keep an even thickness. Keep your stitches firm.

To start and end a thread To end the thread, take the needle into the coil in the usual stitch, but do not come out at the back. Take the needle along the coil for about 2–3 cm (1"–1¼"). This way you bury the thread. Release the needle.

To start again tie a knot in the raffia at the end. Thread the needle and insert it into the top of the coil (at last stitch) and come out at the back of the row (thus completing the last stitch). Your next row will cover the knot.

Stepping up to make a wall or edge Start the row for the wall or edge opposite the first row, i.e. where the first row started after finishing the donut (illustration F). You will finish in the same spot (illustration G). Finish the thread off by wrapping several times around the end of the core of leaves and then take the needle down through several rows and up again. Make sure it is firm before cutting off the thread.

E

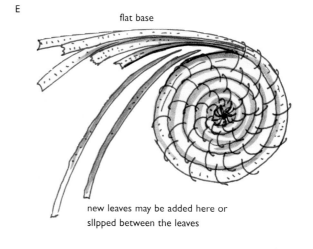

flat base

new leaves may be added here or slipped between the leaves

F

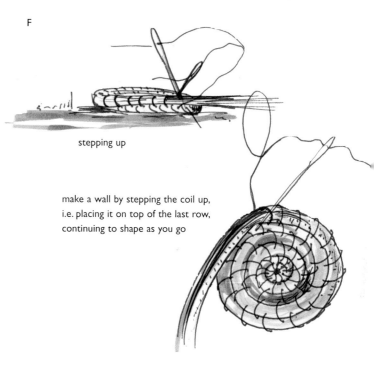

stepping up

make a wall by stepping the coil up, i.e. placing it on top of the last row, continuing to shape as you go

finishing the coil by tapering down to 3 leaves as at the start and securing

G

Ideas . . .

4 dyeing natural materials simply

You can have a fun day playing around with a dyebath. It can be exciting when the colour starts to happen, your adrenaline starts pumping and all sorts of ideas come to mind. You may want to achieve all of them in one day, mind you, but you will very soon learn the discipline that has to come in order to produce.

Yes, it is exciting to dye your materials all the colours of the rainbow with commercial dyes.

BUT—can they be used for the project you have in mind? For example, a 'natural look' for a basket might be the natural colours of your selected materials.

OR—you can dye them to enhance their natural shades by using natural plant dyes or commercial dye. You can brighten a bunch of faded dried leaves by dyeing them a yellow or tan colour. The colour can be controlled by testing a small bundle first. When you think you have the right colour, take it a shade darker, as it will lighten when dry and the colours always look darker when wet.

Wait for dyed material to dry to the 'just damp' state. If you use dyed material straight from the dyebath it will be wet and swollen and as it dries will shrink in your project, leaving it loose and open.

NATURAL PLANT DYES

Many plants contain a useful dye. Natural colours from plants are usually much softer than the colours of commercial dyes and lend themselves beautifully to natural plant fibre projects.

You can extract the colour by boiling the plant material (berries, flowers, leaves, stems, bark, twigs or roots) for half to one hour. Then strain off the liquid. This can be stored in glass jars until you have enough to use, as dye material from flowers, leaves and bark may only become available in small amounts. It is very rare to be able to exactly duplicate a particular colour in natural dyes and preparing dyes is a very time consuming task, but their soft glowing colours are most rewarding.

Best results come from collecting dye materials at specific times. Berries are collected when fully ripe. You can freeze flowers, leaves and berries until you are ready to use them. (Please put a label on the container.) Observe the plants in your garden and note any that show colour in their roots, flowers or leaves. They are worth an experiment so try a dye test.

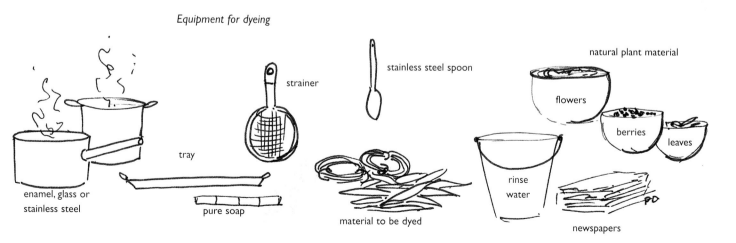

Equipment for dyeing

strainer

stainless steel spoon

natural plant material

flowers

berries

leaves

tray

enamel, glass or stainless steel

pure soap

rinse water

material to be dyed

newspapers

There are many books available on dyeing which mostly give you recipes for dyeing wool, as natural dyes give the most brilliant and lasting colours when used with wool. Fibres of animal origin take dye easily. Cotton and linen are vegetable fibres which are very strong and hard and need careful preparation before they take dye. It is in this more difficult area that we find ourselves when wanting to dye plant material so when you try dyeing keep notes. If you are successful you may be able to repeat the results.

Try corn husks for your first experiments as they take dye very well. Then move on to leaves such as day lily, red-hot poker, iris and grasses.

DYE RECIPES

Use a 3-litre pot in enamel, stainless steel or glass as the dye pot for each recipe. Other materials such as aluminium tend to react with substances in the dye material.

Native hibiscus (*Alogyne huegelii*)

I had fun with the native hibiscus after I noticed that the flowers stained my hands as I took the dead flowers from the bush. So I started collecting daily until I had enough to boil. Within half an hour I had a very good rosy-purple liquid in my pot.

Method
1. Take a large quantity of blue flowers (about half volume of dye pot).
2. Just cover the flowers with water and boil for about half an hour.
3. Strain off liquid.
4. Place dye pot and liquid back on stove to boil and add enough corn husks to stay under the dye liquid. Do not cover the pot.
5. Let liquid come to boil and boil gently for half to one hour.
6. Take out a sample, rinse it in water.
7. If colour is set, remove rest of material, rinse and dry.

Result—a soft pink-garnet shade.

Experiment by adding a quarter to half a teaspoon of bicarbonate of soda in the last half hour. The change can be dramatic, from pink to yellow-green. The same result may be achieved by rinsing in soapy water. Use a pure bar soap. Leave the plant material in the rinse for a minute or two, remove and rinse in clear water.

Blackberries, Aralia berries

Try berries in similar quantities to the hibiscus flowers, but crush them first to release the dye. Follow the instructions for dyeing above. Experiment with any other dark berries you can collect.

Onion skins

Method
1. Save the brown skins until you have a large pot full.
2. Boil for half an hour or more, then strain and use.

Turmeric

Method
1. Place 2 dessertspoons of turmeric powder in one and a half litres of water.
2. Bring to boil.
3. Add the plant fibre.
4. Boil for half an hour. Test a leaf by rinsing.
5. If colour holds, remove leaves, rinse and dry.
   This gives a strong yellow or gold but unfortunately this colour is known to fade quickly in bright light.

COMMERCIAL DYES

You can use a multi-purpose dye, e.g. Dylon, available in small tins from chemist and craft suppliers, on materials such as corn husks, dried leaves, stripped ivy vine.

Method
1. Fill dye pot with 2 litres water.
2. Bring water to the boil.
3. Add half or one package of dye depending on the depth of colour required.

Brown onion skins

Clockwise from left: circular bulrush place mat (page 72); a sculptural piece (page 46); lavender wands (page 69)—note the rubber bands keeping the stalks together until they dry; a wrapped tassel (page 68), and a happy harvest doll (page 67)

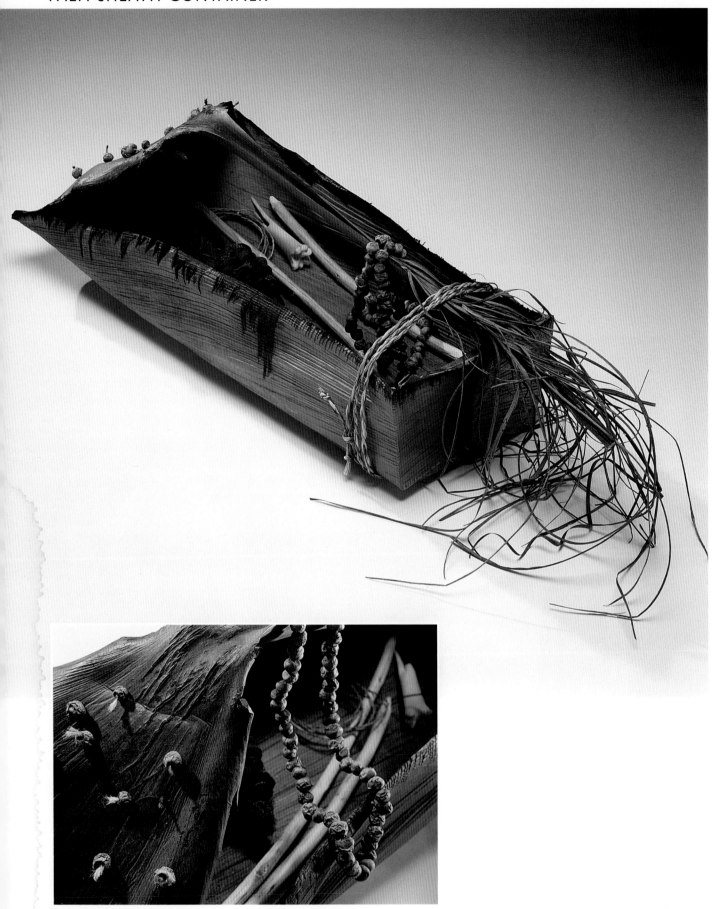

'Container for Survival': palm sheath basket incorporating callistemon pods, banksia seed capsules and twined leaves from various bulbs (detail below)

PLAITED AND SEWN AUTUMN MAT

Plaited with six pieces of the top part of the bulrush, making three pairs, then stitched to make a circular mat (page 73)

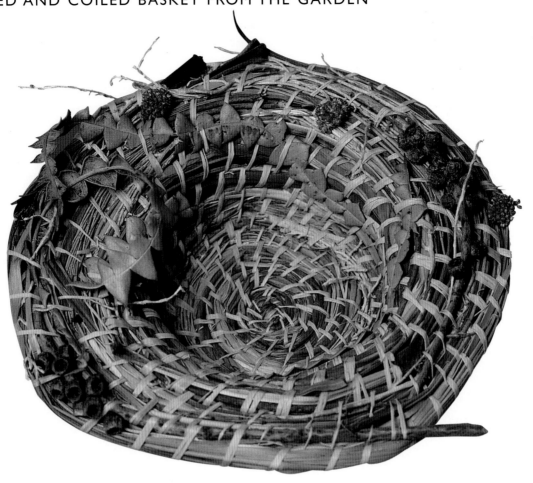

The stitched and coiled basket from my garden described on page 73

4. Add 2 tablespoons liquid dishwashing detergent.
5. Place plant material in boiling solution a few pieces at a time. Do not crowd them.
6. Simmer 15 minutes, stirring occasionally.
7. Drain material and run cold water over it until excess dye is removed.
8. Place dyed material on newspapers to dry until ready to use.

EXHAUST DYEING

Once the first batch of material has been dyed you can add more, just enough to be covered by the dye, and repeat the process. You should finish up with a lighter shade. You may be able to do this three or four times, giving you a range of shades.

EXPERIMENTING WITH COLOUR MIXES

You could try mixing dyes, e.g. yellow and blue to make a green. Add a little brown to dull the colour if it seems too bright.

5 projects you will find e and fun

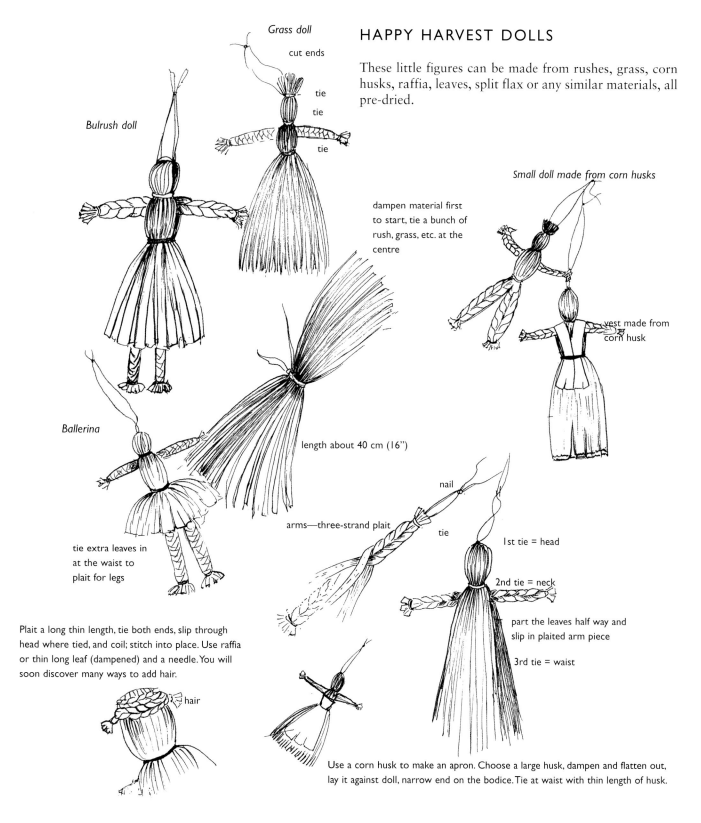

Grass doll

cut ends

tie

tie

tie

Bulrush doll

HAPPY HARVEST DOLLS

These little figures can be made from rushes, grass, corn husks, raffia, leaves, split flax or any similar materials, all pre-dried.

Small doll made from corn husks

dampen material first to start, tie a bunch of rush, grass, etc. at the centre

vest made from corn husk

Ballerina

length about 40 cm (16")

tie extra leaves in at the waist to plait for legs

arms—three-strand plait

nail

tie

1st tie = head

2nd tie = neck

part the leaves half way and slip in plaited arm piece

3rd tie = waist

Plait a long thin length, tie both ends, slip through head where tied, and coil; stitch into place. Use raffia or thin long leaf (dampened) and a needle. You will soon discover many ways to add hair.

hair

Use a corn husk to make an apron. Choose a large husk, dampen and flatten out, lay it against doll, narrow end on the bodice. Tie at waist with thin length of husk.

WRAP A TASSEL

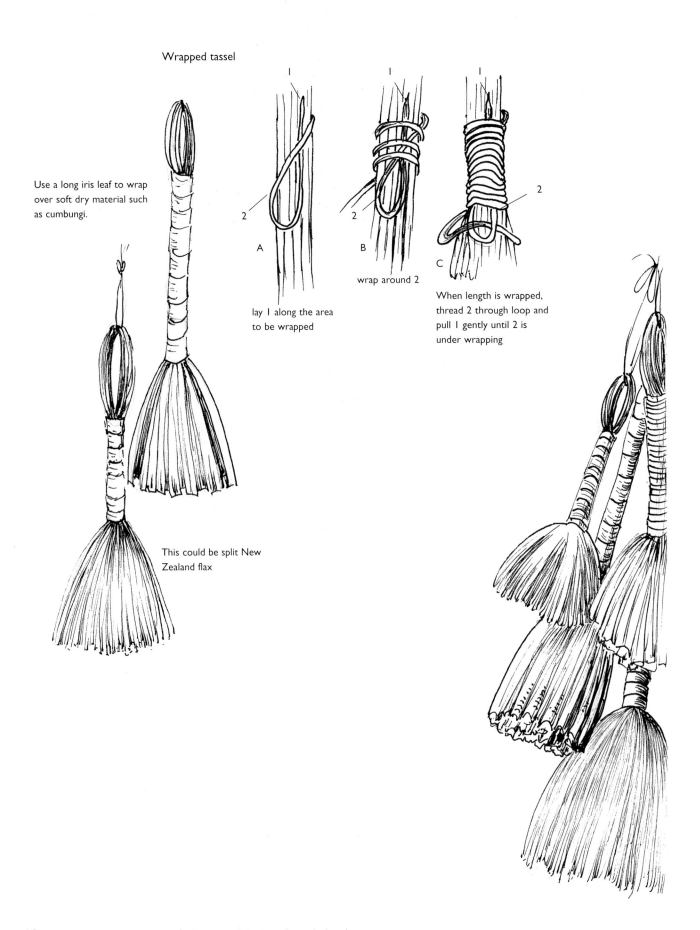

Wrapped tassel

Use a long iris leaf to wrap over soft dry material such as cumbungi.

A

lay I along the area to be wrapped

B

wrap around 2

C

When length is wrapped, thread 2 through loop and pull I gently until 2 is under wrapping

This could be split New Zealand flax

LAVENDER WANDS

Lavender wands, also known as lavender sticks and lavender bottles, are woven.

Weaving over single stems

You will need 15 or 17 succulent stems of freshly cut lavender about 45 mm long. Arrange heads unevenly. Tie tightly with strong cotton or a rubber band and bend stems back one at a time, being careful not to break them (illustration A). The odd number of stems is important for the ribbon weaving. You will need about 1 m (40") of narrow satin or silk ribbon. If a stem or rib (rib is a weaver's term) does break, a substitute can be inserted at stage B (illustration B), tucking one in where the tie is. Fold all stems over the oval bunch of lavender flowers. Begin weaving at the tied end which now becomes the top, tuck one end of ribbon neatly under a couple of ribs and weave over and under each rib with the ribbon (illustration C). Make a downwards spiral as you cover the flowers with the ribbon. Fasten the end of the ribbon with a few stitches after cutting off the excess. Trim ends of ribs evenly across. Tie a length of ribbon into a bow at base of weaving and hold in place with a few stitches (illustration D). Allow to dry for a few days before putting amongst clothes.

Note: If the flower heads on your lavender are large, use fewer stems for the wand.

Weaving over pairs of stems

You will need 9, 11 or 13 pairs of lavender stems with flower heads (in other words, 18, 22 or 26 single stems). Cut stalks as long as possible. You will also need about 2 m (2 yds) of satin, taffeta or silk ribbon 6 mm ($^1/4$") wide, a small elastic band and scissors. If the lavender stems are short, make up 9 pairs to make a smaller wand, and use narrower ribbon.

weaving over one stem

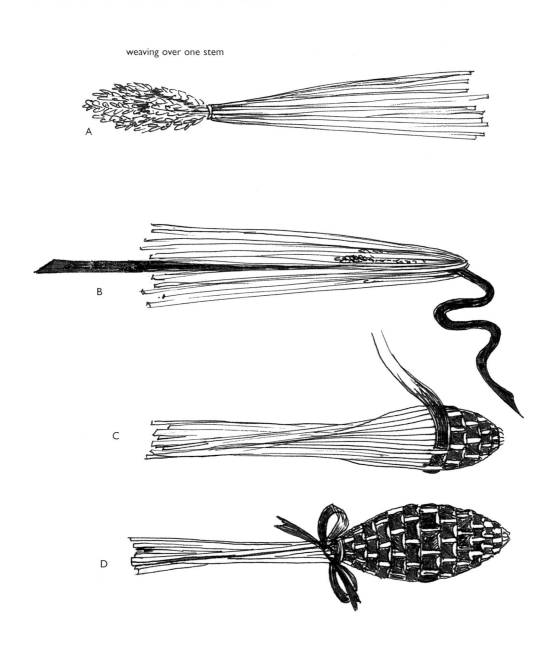

A

B

C

D

Collect stems together with an elastic band pushed up just below the flower heads (illustration A). Tie one end of ribbon below the rubber band and make a firm knot. Turn bunch upside down. Now turn stalks back over the flower heads. Take care with this step as some lavender can be brittle (illustration B). Arrange the stalks in pairs. Tuck the short end of the ribbon into the flower heads and weave over and under pairs of stalks with the long end of the ribbon, adjusting the twists so the ribbon sits nice and flat. Continue until flower heads are right inside the weaving, keep rows firm and even. Wind ribbon once or twice around stalks, pull ribbon through one of the twists to finish. Cut off excess ribbon and make a bow. A bow tied in a wider piece of matching ribbon makes a nice touch.

For varieties of lavender with very fine flowers
Take 21 stems of lavender. Collect together with a rubber band, tie on ribbon, allowing enough on the short end to help make a bow at the finish. Keep this piece inside flowers. Bend over stems, thread long end of ribbon through a bodkin and proceed to weave over and under each single stem, continuing until flowers are covered. Loop off end firmly, retrieve the short end and tie a bow to finish.

THREE PALM SHEATH CONTAINERS

Refer to the information on the Alexandra palm (page 24) for details on the crown shaft.

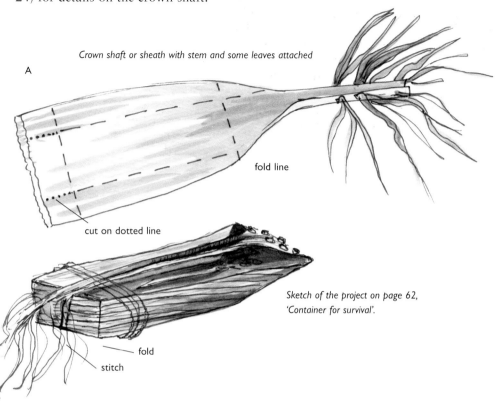

A

Crown shaft or sheath with stem and some leaves attached

fold line

cut on dotted line

Sketch of the project on page 62, 'Container for survival'.

fold

stitch

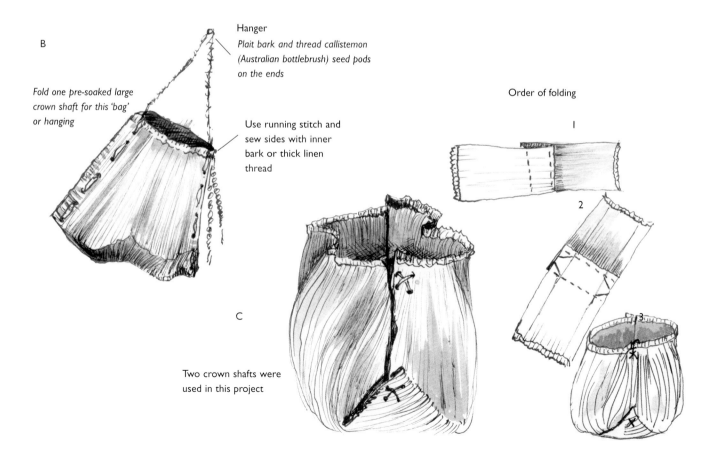

B

Fold one pre-soaked large crown shaft for this 'bag' or hanging

Hanger
Plait bark and thread callistemon (Australian bottlebrush) seed pods on the ends

Use running stitch and sew sides with inner bark or thick linen thread

Order of folding

1

2

3

C

Two crown shafts were used in this project

PLAITED AND SEWN AUTUMN MAT

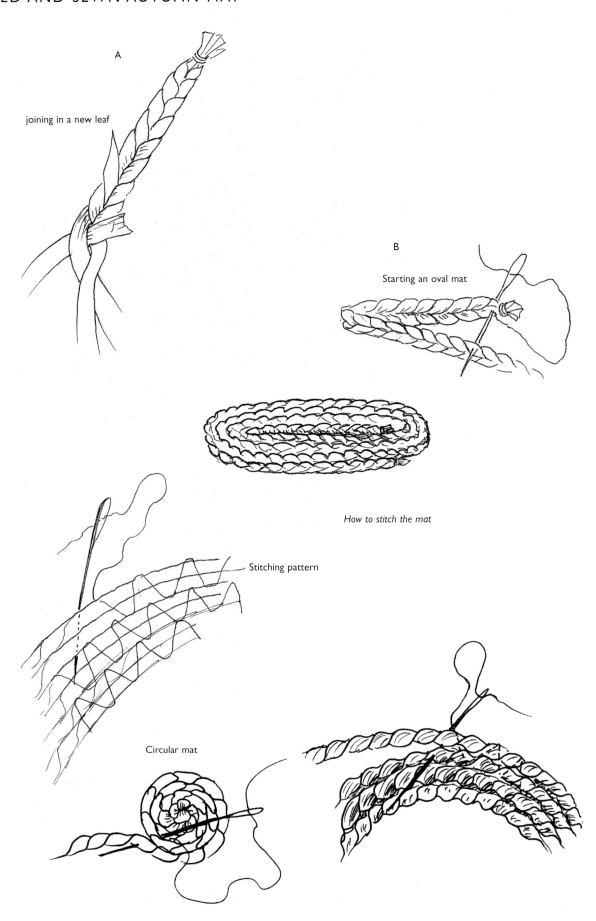

A

joining in a new leaf

B

Starting an oval mat

How to stitch the mat

Stitching pattern

Circular mat

Using this method you can make mats large enough for floor mats or small enough to go on the table.

Large mat with bulrush (cumbungi, cattails)
Autumn is the time to take some friends, a picnic lunch and a pair of scissors out to collect a quantity of long bulrush leaves from your local dam, swamp, stream or drain, and make a mat. At this time of year, many of the outer leaves of the bulrush are dry and soft and you may still find some good green ones to take home to dry for later use (see page 10).

Collecting
Start by collecting the long dry outer leaves. When you have a nice armful of sound material, strip the thin edges off the butt end (the thick end) of the leaves and wipe them down with a damp rag. Select nine leaves (increase the number if you wish to make a larger plait), making three groups. Do not place all the butts together, but alternate them in each group so that your work will be of even, thickness when you begin to plait.

This method can be used to make a set of table mats, using a much thinner plait, e.g. three rushes or six, depending on the thickness of the material available. You may like to use iris leaves or even corn husks instead.

Plaiting
Tie nine leaves all together, then hook the knot around a stump or twig, or tie with a rush and attach to a branch, and begin to plait the three strands as you would if braiding hair, except that you have three leaves crossing three leaves, crossing three leaves. Refer to Braiding or plaiting (page 53) for details.

When you have plaited nearly the full length of the leaves, you will notice that one group is starting to feel a bit thin, or getting a bit shorter. This is where you lay a new leaf or rush on top and continue to plait, doing this with each plait until all nine original lengths have been replaced with new lengths (illustration A). Continue on in this way until you have a very long length of plaited rush. Don't worry about any pieces of rush poking out of the plait where joins have been made. These may be cut off quite safely afterwards, before you start to stitch the mat. Roll the plait into a coil and take it home, where you can stitch it together.

As you were making your length of plait you would have noticed that the material was slightly damp. Freshly collected material in autumn has some natural moisture. This moisture gives the leaves a certain strength and suppleness that allows them to be plaited without breaking. At other seasons you would find for the most part that the leaves are too brittle and break easily.

If your material does become brittle, dampen it. Place it in the bath for ten minutes, then wrap in some damp towels to hold the moisture in, or hose it down on the lawn and cover with damp hessian bags for a few hours or overnight; either way it will become beautifully soft and pliable. Take care not to wet it too much as it will swell and therefore shrink again when dry, with the result that your plait may be loose.

Stitching
You need about 100 metres (110 yards) of plait to make a reasonably sized mat for the floor and 3 metres (10') to make a table mat.

Choose a large needle, e.g. a long slim darning needle, and a strong thread, such as finely split New Zealand flax or a strong linen thread in a natural shade, to sew your mat.

It is a simple matter to stitch the plait together. Start by dampening it. Trim off the untidy ends and firmly fasten the leaves together by wrapping some of the thread firmly around the beginning of the plait (illustration B).

Then with needle and thread stitch the plait together, firstly making sure you are not trying to stitch the plait edge to edge. You will make a stronger mat if the plait is laid against itself so you can only see the side edges on the finished work. You may use any stitch that suits you, making sure that each coil of plait has been stitched to the next.

When the mat is large enough look to see that your rows are even and plan to end the mat in a balanced spot. Stitch over the cut end firmly and make sure that the thread has been firmly attached to the plaiting by pushing the needle back through several rows of plait before you finish it off.

STITCHED AND COILED BASKET FROM THE GARDEN

My garden grows mostly Australian plants with a scattering of exotics. I had the urge to make a basket from all the many textures and shades of greys and browns I saw in the ground litter. So I made a collection:

- Bark strips from the paperbark (*Melaleuca*)
- Twigs of a she-oak—its needles were very long at this time (*Allocasuarina cunninghamiana*)
- Small pieces of *Melaleuca armillaris* with seed capsules included
- Long whippy pieces from the numerous callistemons, along with their beautiful seed pods
- The silver cushion bush (*Calocephalus*) was too silver-grey and beautiful to ignore
- Lavender flowers and their long stems
- Dry cordyline leaves hanging from the stem
- Handful of leaves from a nearby clump of club rush
- Some very large dried leaves around the base of a huge Gymea lily (*Doryanthes excelsa*)—nice and pliable after the rain
- Handful of dried prickly mat rush (*Lomandra longifolia*)

And I had a nice pile. Oh, and the day lilies had some semi-dry leaves just waiting to be collected so in they went as well.

A good deal of this material needed to dry a bit more before I started to stitch, so my creative urge had to be suppressed for several weeks to allow shrinkage to take place. Otherwise the basket would have shrunk within my stitches and become loose as the material dried. By allowing it to dry first your stitching will stay nice and firm.

And so the day came to create . . .
I dipped the day lily leaves in water for a minute or two, wrapped them in a towel to hold their moisture (as I was sitting in the sun and the day was warm). The other material required a longer 'drink', maybe half an hour. Then I threw a damp towel over it also.

I decided to use jute string (from the supermarket) to stitch with, as some of the material was quite strong and would need to be pulled fairly strongly to hold it in place. With the jute threaded into a large-eyed tapestry needle I was ready to start.

I started the coil with the day lily leaves. Nice and soft when damp, they were a good choice to start with.

Method
Take about six leaves, tip ends twisted together, and start the coil, in similar fashion to the picture on page 57. When you have your first round or 'donut', secure it with several firm stitches, then start slipping some other pieces of material in between the day lily leaves so that the core is getting thicker and feeling firmer. You must add material frequently at this stage, every couple of stitches. It should be pencil thickness by the time you have three coils stitched.

Save any twiggy, nutty pieces of material for the walls of the basket and keep the base fairly even so that the basket will sit nicely. Add bits of bark, she-oak needles, lavender stems, fine twigs along with the day lily leaves until you arrive at the thickness of, say, a finger. Stay with this thickness for the whole of the basket. You must always be adding material to keep the coils even—do not forget, or they will be lumpy and bumpy (see Techniques, page 56).

MAKING A GOD'S EYE
This very decorative technique can be used on a basic melon basket at step 3 (page 54). You will need to make two, one for each side. Choose pliable vine or leaves 60–100 cm (24"–50") long—this length makes learning the technique easier.

The vine or leaves may be jasmine, ivy, or pre-dried leaves such as bulrush or red-hot poker that are dampened before use.

Select the best material and have about six lengths beside you, just in case you break a piece. Leaves can be twisted together to make a join.

The ribs of the basket are placed against the god's eye on each end, cut and adjusted as you shape the basket. It is very important to have nice flexible ribs, not twiggy branches.

The god's eye can be worked with handle ring inside or outside the rim of the basket.

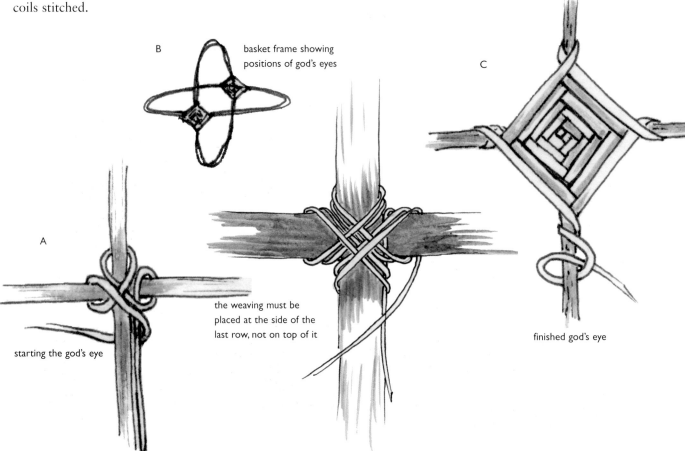

B   basket frame showing positions of god's eyes

C

A

starting the god's eye

the weaving must be placed at the side of the last row, not on top of it

finished god's eye

other useful materials

Refer to Natural materials section for ideas or pre-paration.

FOR MELON BASKET FRAMES

Grapevine—coil into circles and hang to dry for later use
Passionfruit vine—same as grape
Wonga vine (*Pandorea*)—as above
Privet (common hedge plant)—use suckers
Fruit trees (apples, plums)—nice clean growth or suckers

Grasses

FOR WEAVING

Dampen most materials slightly before use.

Banana 'trash'—this is the dried material that hangs from the stem or trunk

Passionfruit vine—finer lengths

Dolichus—creeper, pink-mauve flowers

Choko vine

Melon vine

Sollya

Philodendron sheaths—add excellent colour

Aspidistra leaves—also good for colour

Bulbs (dried daffodil and jonquil leaves)—twist several together as you weave

Watsonia—excellent, good colour

Garlic—the leaves add colour

Parsley—the mature plant when dried

Eucalyptus trees—fibrous bark from some types can be torn away from slab of bark into soft hairy lengths

Muehlenbeckia—black wire-like material

Virginia creeper—use several strands together

FOR COILED BASKETS

Mix materials.

Pine needles—find the long-needled pine tree; collect from the ground

Wild grasses—growing on country roadsides; collect at peak of growth and dry about six weeks

Native grasses (e.g. *Poa* species)—can be harvested from the garden when cutting back in summer

Philodendron sheaths

Watsonia leaves—dried

Garlic leaves

Parsley plant—dried

Daffodil leaves

references

Armstrong, A. *Maori Customs and Crafts* Wellington, Seven Seas Publishing 1981

Australian Institute of Archaeology *Papyrus*, Melbourne 1971

Barratt, O.E. *Basket Making* Doubleday, 1992

Brokensha, P. *The Pitjantjatjara and Their Crafts* The Aboriginal Arts Board Australia Council, Sydney 1978

Carpentier, D. and Bachelet, J. *Basketry* EP Publishing, West Yorkshire 1979

Christopher, F.J. *Basketry* Dover Publications, New York 1952

Cronin, L. Key *Guide to Australian Palms Ferns and Allies* Reed Books, Sydney 1989

Deutch, Y. (ed.) *Basketry for Everyone* Marshall Cavendish, London 1976

Elliot, G. Australian *Plants for Art and Craft* Hyland House, Melbourne 1992

Elliot, W.R. and Jones, D.L. *Encyclopaedia of Australian Plants* Lothian, Melbourne 1990

Everard, B. and Morley, B. *Wildflowers of the World* Octopus Books, London 1973

Friends of Sherbrooke Forest and Department of Conservation Forests & Lands *Weeds of Forests, Roadsides and Gardens*, Melbourne 1989

Gilman, R.S. and Bess, N. *Step by Step Basketry* Golden Press, Sydney 1977

Glasson, M & I. *A Eucalypt Dyers' Handbook*, Carcoar NSW 1980

Hart, C. and D. *Natural Basketry* Watson-Guptill, New York 1978

Herald, J. *World Crafts: Community Aid Abroad* Simon & Schuster, Sydney 1992

Isaacs, J. *Australia's Living Heritage* Lansdowne, Sydney 1984

James G.W. *Indian Basketry* Dover Publications, New York 1972

Keneally, K.F., Choules Edinger, D. and Willing, T. *Broome and Beyond* CALM, Perth 1996

LaPlantz, S. (ed.) *The News Basket*, California 1988

Levitt, D. *Plants and People* Australian Institute of Aboriginal Studies, Canberra 1981

Newman, T.R. *Contemporary South-East Asian Arts and Crafts* Crown Publishers, New York 1977

Puketapu-Hetet, E. *Maori Weaving* Longman Paul, Auckland 1989

Reader's Digest Gardeners' *Encyclopedia of Plants & Flowers*, Sydney 1992

Rees, V. *Seagrass Basketry* Dix Ltd, Perth 1951

Rees, V. *Seagrass Handbags* Dix Ltd, Perth 1950

Rendell, J. *Country Crafts* Routledge & Kegan Paul, London 1977

Richardson, H. (ed.) *Fibre Basketry: Homegrown and Handmade* Kangaroo Press, Sydney 1989

Romanowski, N. *Grasses, Bamboos and Related Plants in Australia* Lothian, Melbourne 1993

Rossbach, E. *The New Basketry* Litton Educational Publishing Inc. New York 1976

Rossbach, E. *Baskets as Textile Art* Litton Educational Publishing Inc. London 1973

Sainty, G.R. and Jacobs, S.W.L. *Water Plants of Australia* Sydney 1994

Scarlett, N.H., Wallbrink, S.J. and McDougall, K. *Native Grasslands* Victoria Press, Melbourne 1992

Sekijima, H. *Basketry* Kodansha International, Tokyo 1986

West, M., Carew, M. and Hughes, A. *Maningrida: The Language of Weaving* Australian Exhibitions Touring Agency, Melbourne 1995

Wightman, G. and Andrews, M. *Bush Tucker Identikit*, Conservation Commission of the Northern Territory, Darwin 1991

Wright, D. *The Complete Book of Baskets and Basketry* David & Charles, London 1977

index

Acacia 28
Agave 9
Arum lily 10
Australian Aboriginal use of plant
    materials 16, 23, 26, 34, 35, 39, 41

Bali 26
Bark 71
    box thorn 27
    hibiscus 27
    inner 33, 34
    ivy 40
    outer 33
    paper 35
    use 48
    wisteria 43
Box thorn 27
Bulrush 8, 10, 46, 73

Callistemons 73
Cane grass 11
Cattail 10
Check weave 11
Clematis 7, 37
Clivia 16
Coiled baskets 56
    materials 10, 11, 12, 13, 14, 15, 16,
    21, 23, 24, 26, 27, 28, 35, 39
Coral pea 38
Cordyline 8, 25, 73
Corn 8, 12
    cobs 12
    corn cob pipes 12
    dolls 12
Cumbungi 8, 10, 73
Cushion bush 73

Day lily 13
Dodder laurel 39
Dyes 59
Dye recipes 60
    aralia berries 60
    blackberries 60
    commercial dye 60
    hibiscus 60
    onion skins 60
    turmeric 60

Elm 33

Fiji 26

Ginger plant 14
Gladiolus 15
God's eye 74
Gymea lily 56

Happy harvest dolls 11, 67
Hibiscus, native 27, 60

Indonesia 26, 39, 43
Iris 8, 15
Ivy 8, 40, 48

Jasmine 8, 40, 48

Kaffir lily 16
Kangaroo paw 16
Kennedia 8, 38
Kurrajong 34

Lavender 28, 73
Lavender wands 28, 69
Lawyer vine 41
Lesser reed-mace 10
Lignum 41
Lignum wreaths 42

Mat rush 16, 73
Mats 72
Melaleuca 73
Melon basket 46, 47, 54–5
    materials 11, 27, 28, 33, 35, 36, 38,
    39, 41, 42, 43, 54

Native Americans 12, 34
Native raspberry 42
New Zealand flax 8, 9, 21, 25, 48
New Zealand Maoris 21

Orchid 13

Pairing weave 11
Pale rush 22
Palm sheath containers 71

Palms 8
    Alexandra 24
    cabbage tree 24
    Lontar 24
    pandanus 26
    rattan 41
Paperbark 35, 73
Plaited and sewn autumn mat 72
Plaiting 73
    materials 10, 11, 12, 13, 16, 22, 24,
    26, 33
Pods 34
Red-hot poker 8, 22
Roots 27, 34, 35

Sculptural piece 46–7
Seaweed 44
Sewing (see Stitching)
She-oak 35, 73
Silks 12
Stitching 73
    materials 11, 13, 14, 15, 21, 22, 73
Suckers 33
Supplejack 37

Tall leaf rush 23
Tassel, wrapped 68
Twining or pairing weave 11, 47
Typha 8, 10

Wait-a-while vine 42
Wattles 28
Wattle-and-daub 28
Wattling 28
Watul 28
Weaver 46, 47
Weaving materials 9, 10, 11, 13, 14,
    21, 22, 23, 24, 25, 26, 27, 33, 34,
    35, 36, 38, 39, 40, 41, 42, 43
Weaving, over and under 11, 46
Willows 8, 36, 48
Wisteria 43
Wrap a tassel 68
Wreaths, materials 11, 39, 41, 42, 43